BOOKS BY ELLEN SWITZER

How Democracy Failed
There Ought to Be a Law
Our Urban Planet

OUR URBAN PLANET

OUR
URBAN

by ELLEN SWITZER

Photographs by
Michael John Switzer
and Jeffrey Gilbert Switzer

ATHENEUM · NEW YORK · 1980

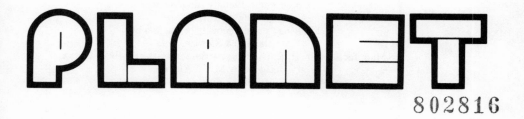

LIBRARY OF CONGRESS CATALOGING IN PUBLICATION DATA

Switzer, Ellen Eichenwald.

Our urban planet.

Includes index.

SUMMARY: Discusses the growth and development
of various types of cities, urban problems and
their solutions, and what the future may hold for cities.
1. Cities and towns—Juvenile literature.
2. City and town life—Juvenile literature.
[1. Cities and towns. 2. City and town life]
I. Switzer, Michael John. II. Switzer, Jeffrey Gilbert.
III. Title.
HT151.S89   307.7′6   80-12225
ISBN 0-689-30788-8

Published simultaneously in Canada by
McClelland & Stewart, Ltd.
Manufactured by R. R. Donnelley & Sons, Crawfordsville, Indiana
Designed by M. M. Ahern
First Edition

To

GILBERT SWITZER

artist, teacher, planner and architect,

who loved many of the world's cities and made

some of them more livable and more

beautiful.

CONTENTS

INTRODUCTION

> City: a large important town.
>
> *Webster's College Dictionary*

I love cities, living in them, working in them, visiting them and learning about their similarities and differences. Over the years, I have made my home in Berlin, Germany; Rome, Italy; Ankara, Turkey; and New York and New Haven, U.S.A.

In the past ten years, it has become increasingly difficult to reconcile how *I feel* about cities with what I am forced *to think* about them. There's no doubt about it: today's cities and the people who live in them face serious problems. Headlines tell us, almost daily, that some of my favorite cities are on the verge of financial and social bankruptcy. All the evils of life in our decade seem to be concentrated in cities: pollution, congestion, overpopulation, poverty, drug abuse and crime. If one mentions such adjectives as "filthy," "sleazy," "run-down," "corruption-ridden," or "teeming," what immediately comes to mind is a street in the large city one knows best.

Some cities seem to be strangling in their own traffic jams. Others are almost buried under a mountain of uncollected garbage and trash. Venice is literally sinking into the water and Mexico City into the ground. Cities seem to get the worst of bad government, and the best and most progressive administrations seem to have run out of ideas on how to solve urban difficulties. And yet, to millions of people throughout the world, cities are still a symbol of hope.

Although some cities (New York, for instance) seem to be losing population, very few city dwellers move into the rural countryside. Instead, they move either to another city or to an area around the city. From the air, some cities look like an ever-expanding doughnut. The center is becoming an empty hole, while the outer edges expand.

What are people looking for when they leave the countryside in which their families have lived for generations and move to large and problem-ridden cities? Everyday life for them seems to get worse, not better. Often they seem to get the worst in housing, education, health care and jobs that their countries have to offer. And yet they rarely return to the rural area they have left. Some governments have tried persuasion and the promise of better homes, education and health care to get families living in squalid huts or tenements in inner cities to go back into the farm country from which they came. Other, more tyranical governments, have forcibly moved people out of the city and back to the country, only to see them come back to the cities as soon as official pressure allowed.

We don't really need statistics to prove to us that we are becoming, increasingly, an urban planet. The astronauts, flying their spaceship far above the globe, may have seen the earth as green and blue: vegetation and water. From an airplane, which gives us a closer view, the earth looks mainly gray and brown by day, black with millions of twinkling lights by night . . . large concentrations of buildings and streets. Of course, we can't see the millions of people who inhabit these building clusters from the air . . . but we know they are there.

In order to find out why cities, in spite of all their problems, seem to attract more and more of the world's people, how city life is similar and/or different in various parts of the world, and how some cities attempt to deal with their most pressing difficulties while others don't, I took a trip around the world in the summer and fall of 1975. I revisited the cities in which I had once lived, to see how they had fared over the years. I also visited some cities I had never seen before and tried to get an impression of the rewards they offered and the difficulties they faced. I interviewed experts in the field of city life: planners, architects, sociologists, mayors and other community leaders. Most important of all, I tried to talk to as many people as I could find who lived and worked in cities, to try to discover what they saw as the problems of urban life and what solutions they might suggest. The fact that I had lived in so many parts of the world helped . . . it meant I could speak to many of these city dwellers in their own language.

I was accompanied on the trip by my son Michael Switzer, a professional photographer, who took most of the pictures in this book, and my daughter-in-law, a former researcher for the Library of Congress, who supplied some of the basic information (*i.e.*, statistics, form of government, etc.) for each chapter. Each morning we would separately go about our work . . . and each evening we would discuss the impressions and information we had gained during the day. Consequently, many of the conclusions reached in this book have been filtered through three minds, rather than just one.

The most important conclusion all three of us reached was that cities, large or small, European, Asian, African or American, all have their share of problems. But they are not, in and of themselves, *the* problem. In even the most frighteningly confused, poverty-stricken, seemingly hopeless urban areas we found a community spirit that seemed to prevail against all difficulties. Everywhere there were creative, vital people: from the policeman walking the beat in London's most crowded slums to the woman physician in New Delhi trying to cope with four times the number of sick and dying that her hospital could hold; from a high city official in Jerusalem who worked with a loaded sub-machine gun slung behind his chair to a home economics teacher in Katmandu teaching the first principles of health and hygene to a class of semi-illiterate girls. These people, of course, did not have ready-made solutions to their city's problem; but all felt that there was no reason to give up hope . . .

that with planning, hard work and a lot of luck their cities might yet be made into places where families might live and someday work in decent and humane surroundings.

None of these people thought that this would be simple. In America we often hear the question: "If we can fly to the moon, why can't we solve the problems of New York?" (or Calcutta, or Ankara, or Venice or Hoboken). In most other parts of the world, where people have lived longer than we have with the problems of decaying and exploding cities, they somehow knew that no technological feat (even one as startling as landing on the moon) would be enough to solve the problems, or even reverse the downward course, of the world's urban areas. But nowhere did we get the feeling that everybody had stopped trying, and that's a re-assuring conclusion to reach. After all, population experts tell us that by the year 2000 more than half of the world's people will be living in cities. It's obvious that we must make city life livable if our green and blue or brown and gray earth is to survive at all.

1

THE CITY

&

HOW IT GREW

1

Our Urban Planet

. . . We are on the verge of one of the most fundamental changes in our history—quite as fundamental as
anything since neolithic man. We are about to switch to an
era on this planet in which there will be more people living
in cities than in the countryside. For the whole of human
history, until our own day, the vast bulk of humanity has
lived on the land, engaged in agriculture; only a minority
lived in the special conditions of city life. And it was felt
to be special. Urbanity, civilization, citizens are all terms
drawn from the idea that man is only civilized if he lives in
the city . . . now the special condition is becoming general, and by the year 2000, urban people—counting as urban
those who live in settlements of more than 20,000—will be
in the majority.

Barbara Ward, one of the world's
outstanding economists and environ-
mentalists, in the 11th annual Gropius
lecture at Harvard University in 1973

Why don't we just sell it to the Arab oil shieks?

A sarcastic remark made by William
Simon, U.S. Secretary of the Treasury
in 1975, when he was asked how he
would suggest solving the enormous
human, social and economic prob-
lems of New York City

As long as anyone has been recording the history of mankind, we have lived in a love–hate relationship with our

cities. As Barbara Ward indicates, the words "urbanity" (meaning polite or suave), "civilization," and even "citizen" originate in the word and concept of "city." Athens is our model for culture and art. Rome reminds us of early architecture and engineering. Even more telling is the image of Jerusalem (a city in which the explosion of terrorist bombs is now an almost weekly occurrence) as a sort of spiritual home. Hymns and spirituals speak of Jerusalem as a symbol of heavenly places to come. The prophets spoke of the vision of cities with gates of amethyst and pearl, and gates of gold. The city gave promise of paradise. On the other hand, the barbarians lived in the rural countryside, where urbanity and civilization had not yet reached.

But even in the Bible there is an entirely opposite picture of cities. Sodom and Gomorrah were so filled with vice and corruption that God decided that they had to be wiped off the face of the earth. Babylon became a symbol of treachery and evil. And when a United States government official talks of "selling New York to the Arab Oil shieks," a lot of Americans smile approvingly. Of course, they wouldn't think of actually offering the shieks (or anyone else for that matter) their largest, most famous city, the "Big Apple," which every artist, musician, dress designer or stock broker tries to reach. But then again, wouldn't it be easier to have someone else worry about all those muggings, those overcrowded and dirty subways, the millions of families living in slums on welfare, the pollution, the piled-up garbage—and the everlasting debts? To many of us, New York, and many of the world's other large cities, are "a great place to visit—but we wouldn't want to live there."

Today, about one and a half billion people live in cities. Economists predict that by the year 2000 the critical reversal will have taken place: three and a half to four billion people will be city dwellers and only three billion will live in the country. We will truly have become an urban planet. How and why is this happening, especially since so many of us look at cities as the places where crime stalks the streets and corrupts the local government; while so many of our writers, journalists and poets are telling us about the clean, green countryside, where our fellow citizens are good neighbors and our politicians honest men and women?

For some of the answers we have to look at history and the development of cities in the past. In the first chapters of this book we will look at the world's great cities and how they came to grow and thrive. We will also look at others that seemed to grow quickly and then vanished, almost as quickly. What was the difference between an urban community that lived through the centuries and one that couldn't even withstand a few decades?

There are different kinds of cities, established for different purposes, whether these cities are called Washington, D.C., Bonn, Germany, Brasilia, Brazil, or Ankara, Turkey. And cities have similar problems. On a recent Sunday, the *New York Times* carried two three-column headlines on its front page. One of the headlines reminded New Yorkers that, unless something drastic happened, New York City was rapidly going broke, could not pay its present debts, and would have to fire more than forty-one thousand employees by July 1. Most of them would be policemen, firemen and hospital workers at a time when crime figures were increasing with depressing monthly regularity; fires— apparently deliberately set by discouraged landowners or youthful gangs—were breaking out almost daily in the Bronx—one of the city's boroughs; and there were constant complaints that very sick people were waiting for hours in overcrowded city hospital emergency rooms for treatment because there were not enough doctors and nurses on the city's payroll.

Another *New York Times'* story was headlined: "ROME ALSO STAGGERS UNDER BURDEN OF DEBT" and began: "Rome, the congested, problem-ridden capital of a nation that has just had a close brush with bankruptcy, is gasping for survival beneath billions of dollars of debt." In Rome, too, firemen and policemen were being dismissed, city hospitals were being closed, and garbage was piling up in the streets.

One week later the *New York Times* front page headline read: "LONDON SHAKY DESPITE AID THAT EXCEEDS NEW YORK'S. Illtyd Harrington is a fiercely bearded Welshman, the second most powerful man in London's government, and the owner of an impressive pair of gold cufflinks embossed with New York City's seal (a gift from his opposite number, Deputy Mayor of New York, James Cavanagh*). A few weeks ago he was thinking of sending them back. Now he is keeping them because New York has managed to postpone bankruptcy. Mr. Harrington and the city he helps run have problems of their own . . . It's bureaucratic machinery, while simpler than New York's, is cumbersome. Wages and other municipal costs are soaring, and local debts have nearly doubled in the last year."

Earlier, London, Rome and Paris were crippled by city-wide strikes of municipal workers who allowed mountains of garbage and trash to collect in the streets. Rats and roaches that had formerly made their homes in the slums of these cities were migrating to the best neighborhoods. And the inhabitants of these neighborhoods were thinking of migrating somewhere else . . . anywhere where problems looked smaller and, therefore, might be solved more easily.

Yet, London stockbrokers, French wine merchants and New York advertising copy writers were not moving to rural communes in the middle of a cornfield. They might move to suburbs . . . but these are really part of a city. What this kind of movement does is to spread the land area of the city further . . . it does not decrease the population, nor solve or even relieve the problems. And so with people moving in and people only seeming to move out, the movement toward a more urban planet continues.

Even if we wanted to, we can't sell New York to the oil sheiks. They are not in the market for it—they have their own fast-growing capitals to worry about.

* Cavanagh was retired from his post shortly thereafter.

2

In the Beginning ...

Human life swings between two poles: movement and settlement.

Lewis Mumford in *The City in History.*

We cannot know where and when humankind changed from nomads to settlers, nor when enough settlers congregated in one place to make up the first village. Urban historian Lewis Mumford thinks that the roots of settlement may lie in our animal past.

He points out that many creatures, including even fish, the lowest on the developmental scale, came together in herds and schools to mate and to rear their young. Birds sometimes return to the same nest from season to season. Those swallows that keep coming back to the mission buildings in Capistrano, California, may be following the same instinct that drives twentieth century humans to seek sunny hot climates (in Florida or the Caribbean) during the coldest part of the winter, only to return to more northern, cooler climates in the hottest part of the summer. Other birds have their own "territories," where they build their nests and defend them against others of their own species.

"Even the technological complexity of the human town does not lack animal precepts," Mumford writes. "Beavers, for instance, go about deliberately making their own environment. They fell small trees and build dams and lodges. If the beaver colony lacks many of the attributes of a town, it is already close to those early villages that also performed feats of hydraulic engineering."

Insects not only build structures, they even form primitive societies. The structure of an anthill or a beehive is close to that of our earliest towns and cities. Even the division of labor, the differentiation of castes, the practice of war, the institution of royalty, the domestication of other species, and the employment of slavery existed in certain ant colonies, probably millions of years before the same ideas and practices could be found in an ancient city.

Mumford points out that although we do find certain similiarities between these animal and human settlements, there is one vast difference. Even in the most primitive settlements, there is evidence that our human ancestors had an awareness of death. "Soon after one picks up man's trail in the earliest campfire or chipped stone tool, one finds evidence of interests and anxieties that have no animal counterpart," he writes. "In particular, a ceremonious concern for the dead, manifested in their deliberate burial . . . with growing evidence of pious apprehension and dread . . . mid the uneasy wanderings of paleolithic man, the dead were the first to have a permanent dwelling."

Mumford and other researchers theorize that burial mounds and caves were landmarks to which a wandering tribe returned at intervals. "The first greeting of a traveler, as he approached one of the ancient cities of Rome and Greece, was a row of graves and tombstones that lined the roads to the city." As for Egypt, the most important buildings left of that great civilization are the pyramids, tombs for Egyptian royalty.

Mumford speculates that, along with the knowledge of their own mortality, primitive tribes developed myths and religious practices to keep death at bay. So, along with graves, archeologists have found evidence of temples or ceremonial places in the very earliest human habitation.

"In the earliest gathering about a grave or a painted symbol, a great stone, or a sacred grove, one has the beginning of a succession of civic institutions that range from the temple to the astronomical observatory, from the theater to the university," Mumford writes.

He has another interesting theory: "Certainly 'home and mother' are written over every phase of neolithic agriculture, and not in the least over the new village centers," he maintains. In his opinion, women wielded "the digging stick and the hoe, tended the garden crops and accomplished those masterpieces of selection and cross-fertilization, which turned raw wild species into the prolific and richly nutritious domestic varieties. They also made the first containers, either by weaving baskets or forming clay pots. Without containers to collect more than one day's food and water, a permanent settlement was impossible. And as the containers became larger (from pot to oven, to grain bin and cistern) settlements became almost inevitable. The containers were simply too heavy to carry along."

Once permanent settlements were formed, walls apparently were built around them to keep woman and children safe from marauding tribes and wild animals. For prehistoric people, child care was apparently a task for the whole community. During the hunting, growing and harvesting seasons, all the adults in the primitive settlement had to work. Older children took care of younger ones. This same pattern can still be seen in agricultural areas throughout the world.

The dog and the pig were apparently the first animals domesticated by the early villagers. The dog was used for hunting, as a guard, and as a scavenger. "It is doubtful that without the dog and the pig, the close-packed community could have survived," Mumford writes. ". . . the pig served as an auxillary department of sanitation right into the nineteenth century, in supposedly progressive towns like New York and Manchester." When grain became plentiful enough to be stored, cats were added to the primitive households to keep rodents away.

The earliest settlement, probably constructed in the Near East between 11,000 and 9000 B.C., was probably a group of mud huts, a little like the beaver's lodge. Around ancient villages were garden plots and patches. Nearby there was always a swamp or a river. Even in the most primitive hamlets, houses contained a jar, sunk into the floor, to catch rainwater. Without water, there was no life. Drought was the fiercest enemy of the early settlers, more dangerous even than starvation or disease. There also was probably some kind of shrine, built over the graves of the villagers' ancestors.

Anthropologists also speculate that as the settlement grew, some sort of governing body was probably established. Since there was no written language, rules and regulations that had worked in the past had to be communicated through spoken words. In a culture without books and records, only the aged have had enough time to learn all that has been discovered over the years, and so it is assumed that the oldest men and women made up the governing body. This is still true in village communities of Africa, Asia and South America. It was also true for American Indian tribes. "The elders personified the hoarded wisdom of the community; all participated, all conformed, all joined in restoring order. . . ." Mumford writes.

The ancient Greeks thought that their own respect for custom and common law, as opposed to the whims of tyrants, was unique in their culture. Our own concepts of law come to us from the Greeks. But actually, democracy was probably the form of government in the earliest settlements of mankind . . . not because it was morally the right form of government, but because it was the only one that *worked*.

The first human settlements probably continued in much the same form for thousands of years. Anthropologists and archeologists speculate that the invention of the wheel may have made it possible to expand these small settlements into towns. The wheel made it possible to harvest more crops, further removed from the settlement's outer borders. More grain and water was stored for future use. For the first time, these communities had goods that needed to be protected from members of other settlements. So, towns were built to be defended, often at the top of a hill with moats and trenches around them. Fields and gardens would then be outside the walls, which meant that in order to plow the fields and sow and harvest the crops, those who lived in the town had to walk farther and farther to do their work.

Many historians think that at the time the villages became towns, people first started to think of work as something that had to be distinguished from the other activities of the day. In the earliest settlements, everybody just gathered enough food and collected enough water for day-to-day survival. In the larger towns, historians speculate that some of the stronger, more able inhabitants probably gathered more grain than they themselves could consume. So they bartered grain for the labor of others less able or less fortunate. And since sowing and harvesting, hunting, building and pot-making were no longer cooperative activities, a system of taskmasters and workers developed.

The new, more varied and larger communities also became more difficult to govern. For one thing, different citizens now had different interests. Those who used goods to extract services from others wanted to make sure that they held on to those goods. One can assume that those who had become paid workers may sometimes have been envious and occasionally downright angry at those who had much more leisure. To keep the town in some kind of order, the Council of Elders, which had only persuasive powers, probably was no longer practical. It is probable that the citizens elected their first chieftain or king at a time when disorder threatened the settlement, or when it was attacked by another group of men and a planned defense became necessary. Once that chieftain was in power, he became very difficult to dislodge. He had probably been selected, in the first place, because he was the most competent soldier, and he had gathered other soldiers around him to protect the village. In exchange for promising the citizens protection from invasion, he expected tributes in the form of goods and obedience. Where, in the early village, everyone had been equal, a new ruling class began to emerge.

Some of the new rulers were worshiped as gods by

their subjects. It seemed only logical that the man who could protect them from their human and animal enemies might also be able to guard them against natural disasters: storms, floods, earthquakes and droughts.

When all that happened, Mumford writes, the village culture "yielded to the urban 'civilization,' that peculiar combination of creativity and control, of expression and repression, of tension and release, whose outward manifestations had been the historic city."

In order to become "citizens," our ancestors had to sacrifice some freedom to obtain order, some independence for protection, some individuality for convenience. Those cities that were best able to live with all these contradictions flourished. Those that could not come to terms with them probably died . . . early in the dawn of history.

3

Why Cities?

New York is the concentrate of art and commerce and sport and religion and entertainment, bringing to a single compact area the gladiator, the evangelist, the promoter, the actor, the trader and the merchant.

E. B. White

Author E. B. White has put his literary finger on one reason why so many of us live in cities. We love the variety they offer. They give us opportunities to work in many different fields and to have fun in many ways.

Actually, when we look at history, the variety in work opportunities was probably the first reason why isolated farms turned into small settlements, settlements turned into larger communities, and then into huge cities.

Mr. Caveman and his wife and family were almost entirely dependent upon their own skills and hard work to survive. They might sometimes have had to look for assistance from their nearest neighbor, but he was often a day's walk away. That meant that each family had to produce everything it might need. They had to hunt for animals to provide meat for food and furs for clothing. They looked for berries and herbs to supplement their diet. They had to find their own cave or build their own shelter with materials close enough to their proposed homes so that the rocks and boulders could be carried into place. If they had to buy goods and services they could not produce themselves, they had to barter with their nearest neighbors: an animal skin for a bowl of grain, assistance in building a shelter for assistance in organizing a hunt. But distances made such barter difficult.

All that independence had advantages. Many of to-day's young people look back at it longingly, and try to establish themselves in the few isolated spots that are still available on this earth to imitate the life style of our remote ancestors. But, judging by history, that life style did not really suit the majority of those who had to live it. They sought a different way of life . . . and they found it, by moving closer together.

There is one obvious reason for this desire to share one's life with others and to pool one's resources. The small group of people who lived in isolation had no choice when it came to daily activities. They *had* to search or hunt for food. They had to make spears and arrowheads for the hunt. They had to turn furs into clothing. They *had* to chop trees and drag stones and pile them on top of each other for shelter. They *had* to move when animals or growing things became less plentiful in their area. Even though our earliest ancestors could not write and, therefore, could not leave us a record of how they lived, we know from our own experience that some were probably more interested and talented in one activity than in another and that few enjoyed or were able to do *everything* that was required to survive. They were bound to look for choices, and they did.

So the hunter, or later the nomad herdsman, who was perhaps an exceedingly able builder, but not very good at hunting or herding, heard of settlements where houses went up by the dozens, instead of one at a time. There that person could devote his talents to building . . . and count on someone else to do the hunting or herding, or in the settlement, the plowing and sowing. The builder could exchange his labor for that of another person living close by who was able and eager to do the things he disliked and at which he usually failed. A woman might be an excellent spinner or weaver, but untalented and uninterested in preserving food. If she moved from an isolated living place to a village, town or city, she too would be able to concentrate on spinning, not only her own but other families' wool, while another person preserved the food that always spoiled when she attempted to preserve it.

In settlements and communities people could pool their talents and abilities, and the results were usually better-built homes, more colorful and more durable cloth, and less famine because crops were raised not simply gathered.

What's more, there was protection in numbers. And isolated family could be wiped out by forces of nature over which they had no control. The fear of such a disaster was always with them. Then there were other people, perhaps a larger, stronger family, or even a wandering group of families, who might want to take over, and against whom they were totally defenseless. Living with other families tended to frighten off small groups of invaders and gave one at least a fighting chance to protect oneself against a larger group.

Also, as people pooled their talents and some of their resources, they found that there was always someone who had an idea of how to do the necessary work more easily and more quickly. The inventors and innovators were able to share their knowledge and skills with friends and neighbors. Life in the larger settlements became easier and more prosperous than life alone in the wilderness.

People also looked for entertainment, fun and laughter, and more often than not found it with each other. There was the woman who could sing songs about life and love and pain and joy. There was the man who could make up marvelous stories about heroes and cowards, about real and imaginary events. Someone could make instruments or invent games that could be played. When the sun went down at night, one could get together with one's neighbors for a good time, instead of just going to sleep because there was nothing else to do.

When a new baby was born, there was usually a woman in the settlement who was particularly talented at making labor and childbirth easier for her neighbors. When someone got sick, there might be someone who knew about herbs, poultices and other "medicines" that would help to cure the patient. And when someone died, there were neighbors to help bury the dead and comfort those still living. Early history shows us that many people must have found life in larger and larger settlements easier, more productive and more entertaining than living in isolated families. At least there is a trend, as old as recorded history, towards communal living and away from isolation.

Settlements that were located in particularly advantageous spots grew faster. The community on the river, which made the transportation of food from the countryside possible, became a center of trade. The community that was surrounded by particularly rich agricultural land became a center of population—because it could feed more people. The community that had a ruling class interested in music and poetry and architecture became a center of culture. And the city that had a particularly strong ruler (often a tyrant) who had military abilities and could build conquering armies, often became a center of government. Archeologists have noted that when the city of one civilization died because of plague, war or natural disaster, another city was often built on the same spot, right on top of the ruins of the old one. Obviously, the location itself was particularly advantageous for city life.

Cities grew slowly but steadily through the ages. Some, like Athens, Rome, Peking and Jerusalem became centers of whole civilizations, of ways of life based on a particular philosophy of government and religion, as well as architecture, art and literature. Sometimes when the city no longer served as a center of population, its philosophy and artistic accomplishments continued to influence later generations.

The growth of cities was slow and steady through the Middle Ages until the end of the eighteenth century and the beginning of the nineteenth, then a drastic change occurred that turned the trickle of newcomers to the urban places into a stream. That change is known as the industrial revolution.

In earlier times, a few tradesmen, craftsmen and

artisans might have combined their talents and efforts to manufacture more of a given item than each could have accomplished alone. However, with the industrial revolution came the factory. The factory made not dozens but thousands of items, and those who worked there often did not need any special skill outside of running a machine, which could be learned in a few days. For the first time, city dwellers began to recruit others to join them, including some who did not have the special talents or skills that previously had been needed for city life.

In the Middle Ages, the poor drifter who wandered into a city without any visible means of support or marketable skills was often put in a workhouse where he chopped wood from dawn to dusk. The citizens hoped he would soon decide to go back to where he came from. Or he might just be escorted unceremoniously to the outskirts of town and told not to return. Now, an unskilled drifter, with a little effort, could be turned into a valuable factory hand. Of course, his life might be very unpleasant. During the industrial revolution, cities were not exactly the places of pearls and gold described by the prophets. Far from being centers of light, peace and enjoyment, they were often filthy, disease-ridden, noisy and filled with pressure and misery. This fact the recruiters for the cotton mills of Liverpool, England, or the shoe factories of Boston, Massachusetts, did not bother to tell the country folk whom they lured into town with promises of good wages, better living conditions, and more fun and recreation.

We see a picture of the nineteenth century city in great French novels by Balzac and Zola, and in English novels by Dickens; Paris and London certainly sound like places that any sensible human being would want to avoid. Gangs of children, the ones who did not work from dawn to dusk in dank, dark, unsafe factories, roamed the streets and often stole for a living. The punishment for stealing was severe: usually hanging, even if the item stolen was a loaf of bread and the thief ten years old. The aged, who had held an accepted and respected place on the farm or in the small

City Symbols

The Sphinx and the Pyramids have survived centuries of
sandstorms, earthquakes and other disasters. They may not
survive the next fifty years intact, however, because the
acrid smoke from industrial Cairo is eating away the
Sphinx's face.

London's Picadilly Square has become a gathering place for young tourists from all over the world. It's one of the best spots for a traveler to gather useful information on inexpensive hotels, restaurants and entertainment for all of Europe.

Below: Once tourists and airlines discover the beauty of Nepal, this scene may become as familiar as the Eiffel Tower in Paris. It's the Monkey Temple in Katmandu.

Right: The baroque market in Bonn. The square is no longer typical of the new capital of Germany, however. Most of Bonn now looks like the typical instant city . . . right out of an American architectural magazine. German Information Center

Pages 22–23: Old Stockholm could double as a movie set for Camelot. New Stockholm looks more like a set for *Star Trek*. Swedish Information Service

Above: The Cathedral of Notre Dame in Paris. French Embassy Press and Information Division

Right: Some cities can be recognized by looking at one symbolic building: for instance, the large mosque (formerly a Greek Orthodox church called St. Sophia) that dominates the cityscape of Istanbul.

Left: Tokyo's Ginza is as much a landmark as New York's Times Square. It's a lot cleaner and safer, however.

Below: A forest of television antennas definitely does not add to the beauty of Jerusalem's temples. Even the finest historical landmarks can be scarred by twentieth century technology and architecture.

rural community, were often left to their own devices in the city. Instead of rocking in the sun or sitting by the fireside in the old homestead, they often were sent to almshouses where poor treatment, bad nutrition and exposure to heat and cold usually hastened their deaths. The nineteenth century city, whether it was located in Europe or in America or in Asia was not a place for the poor and unresourceful. It was meant for the rich, the active, the intelligent and, all too often, the unscrupulous.

But it was possible in this new city of this new age to escape the class into which one had been born. The poor farmer or peasant with industry, and especially, with good luck, could become a rich factory manager. His son could become an aristocrat if the family managed to amass enough fortune in one or two generations. This had not been possible before. Many of these fortunes were made out of the misery of one's fellowman, with little scruple. Poverty and sickness were considered to be more of a disgrace than a misfortune; and very little was done, by the government or by organized religion or by individuals, to help those who were among the least fortunate of the city dwellers. Yet, again, there was no rush to return from the city to the countryside. Most of those who had moved to cities from rural areas stayed in their new homes, overcrowded, miserable and filthy as they might be.

Those who did leave were the rich and powerful who, seeing that the centers of cities were becoming disagreeable places to live, moved to the outskirts. The movement to the suburbs is nothing new; it began with the industrial revolution. The early part of the nineteenth century saw the beginning of the abandonment of inner cities by those who could afford to get away. First they went as far as carriages would allow them to commute to their daily jobs, which were, of course, still in the city. Later they went as far as trains and automobiles could take them.

"This process of establishing an urban system by trying to escape from it started in the nineteenth century, and there is no denying that the movement was a reflection of the extreme discomfort of living in urban turmoil and industrial filth and unrest," says Barbara Ward. The whole movement is continuing . . . to the point where a coastal strip between Boston and Florida has become one vast industrial and residential sprawl . . . and so has a strip of land along the Adriatic and the Mediterranean coastline.

As in the past, in the future, possibilities for work and recreation will take more and more of us to cities or to suburbs, which are really parts of cities. We may dream of the peace of green fields with singing birds and colorful flowers, but our home will be on a paved, busy street . . . with many different kinds of neighbors. From past history and present experience of city dwellers throughout the world, we shall have to learn how to make our cities at least livable and, at best, pleasant. What can we do about the vast and seemingly insoluable problems that cities present? Can the experience of other cities teach us to plan for a better, more productive and less dangerous city life? What has gone wrong with some cities and right with others, and why?

4

Why Cities Grow and Some Grow Old and Die

Some cities are really successful, and present a solid and definite achievement of the thing at which their builders aimed; and when they do this, they present, just as a fine statue presents, something of the direct divinity of man, something immeasurably superior to mere nature, to mere common mountains, to mere vulgar seas.

The modern city is ugly, not because it is a city, but because it is not enough of a city, because it is a jungle, because it is confused and archaic, surging with materialistic energies. In short, the modern town may be offensive because it is a great deal too like nature, a great deal too like the country.

G. K. Chesterton

Born of a railroad, Atlanta grew as its railroads grew. With the completion of four lines, Atlanta was now connected with the West, with the South, with the Coast, and through Augusta, with the North and the East. It had become the crossroads of travel north and south and east and west, and the little village leaped to life.

". . . Why was this place so different from other Georgia towns? Why did it grow so fast? After all, they thought that

it had nothing whatever to recommend it . . . only the railroads and a bunch of mighty pushy people.

Margaret Mitchell in *Gone With The Wind*

Margaret Mitchell's ideas of why some cities grow and
flourish, while others wither and die, is a great deal more
realistic than G. K. Chesterton's. Some of the ugliest cities
in the world are also our most flourishing urban centers.
Some of the most lovely are maintained almost exclusively
as museums, like Venice; and others have become three-
star spots in tourist guidebooks, like Chartres, France,
where once kings and emperors were crowned but which
now has at least five souvenir stands per block.

Some rural legislators and certain TV revival preachers would have us believe that cities have died because
of the immorality and permissiveness of their rulers or
inhabitants. This is demonstrably untrue. Athens, for instance, died as the political and cultural capital of the
world, not because of the poor behavior of its citizens, but
because other nations, especially the Roman Empire, were
able and willing to devote their resources to war rather
than to peace. And the Roman Empire collapsed not because of the orgies in the temples of Bacchus, but because
the Barbarian tribes to the North managed to get themselves organized. There were simply more Barbarians than
Romans . . . and once the former decided to make common cause against a common enemy, Rome was doomed as
the capital of the world. Anthropologists and archeologists
tell us, however, that the Barbarians had morals and customs that would have made the most corrupt Roman emperor blush.

So what makes a city rise from obscurity and flourish
for centuries? In a way, Margaret Mitchell's statement
about Atlanta before the Civil War is applicable to many
of the flourishing cities of the world. What's important

are often two factors: location and "mighty pushy people," plus a few accidents of history.

Railroads no longer determine the prosperity of a city or a region. Airlines and highways have taken their place. But Atlanta has been able to adapt to the change. It's still one of the most prosperous, growing cities of the American South—and has one of the most modern, efficient international airports in the world. Other cities in the United States and the world also have excellent airport facilities, but Atlanta was among the first to realize that with the decline of railroads air traffic was becoming one of the most important factors in the growth of a city. So, Atlanta's "mighty pushy people" saw to it that, early on, funds were directed towards building an airport that could serve the entire South.

Dallas and Houston, Texas, also have made considerable efforts toward further growth and prosperity, and both cities have been noticeably successful in establishing themselves as major urban centers in a period of less than fifty years. Whatever it took to attract business and industry, the city fathers in Texas promoted. From football stadiums to hospitals, from theaters to banks, the pushy Texans provided. Today, the rich and famous from all over the world come to Houston for business and entertainment. The Astrodome, with its artificial green turf, has become a world monument, a symbol of instant prosperity. The most renowned surgeons now practice in Houston, not in Vienna or London. And Dallas has the only theater in the world designed by this century's most outstanding architect, Frank Lloyd Wright, paid for, in part, by city money. Of course, an accident of history and geography has helped. It's clear that Texas cities would not have enjoyed their spectacular growth had it not been for all those oilwells that dot the nearby landscape. But there are even more oilwells in Saudi Arabia, and somehow Ryadah, the capital of the Saudis, has not yet become a household word. In fact, it difficult to find out anything about that city at all . . . only the most recent edition of the Encyclopaedia Britannica contains a few short paragraphs about its development. Ryadah may be the headquarters of dozens of international oil companies, but it has not yet established the equivalent of a Chamber of Commerce.

So cities grow because people and circumstances— location, politics and adaptation to conditions—make them grow. And they die because the things that make them grow disappear or lose their usefulness.

An almost perfect example of how a city can rise to preeminence because of accidents of history and geography, and then fall into an irreversible decline is Venice, called by some the most beautiful place on the face of the earth. Today Venice is a museum city. (See Chapter 18.)

Other lovely Italian cities seem to be following the same historical route as Venice. Until fairly recently Florence, for instance, could still be considered a manufacturing center as well as a tourist attraction. But several years ago, floods wiped out the shoe and handbag factories and the knitting mills that provided opportunities for industrial employment for its citizens. Many of these factories were not rebuilt, although its churches, bridges and palaces were. Italian wages have never been up to the wages earned by workers in many other European countries, but they still outpaced those paid in Spain and Portugal, as well as in some of the Oriental cities that had begun to manufacture leather goods. Italian shoes and handbags simply got to be too expensive. Now only a very few of the factories are still in operation. These make high-priced merchandise for some of the most expensive stores in the world and also those hand-tooled leather wallets and key rings that are sold in Florence to (you guessed it) tourists.

Some cities, as they approached the end of their usefulness as industrial or transportation centers, decided voluntarily to turn themselves into museums or entertainment centers. Salzburg, Austria, is a perfect example. Salzburg is a charming, middle-sized city located on a river, with a castle overlooking some well-preserved medieval streets. In addition to the castle on the hill, Salzburg also has two lovely eighteenth century palaces. But there are many other attractive European cities with palaces and medieval streets in Europe, so these features were not enough to assure a tourist boom. About seventy-five years ago, the city fathers had an inspiration: Let's use the fact that the great composer Wolfgang Amadeus Mozart was born here to start an annual Mozart festival. After all, the castle's ballrooms were ideal for concerts. They needed only a few electric lights and a little renovation. A volunteer organization took on the task of promoting the summer concerts, with artists drawn from the faculty of the outstanding music school that was already one of the city's assets. So the summer Saltzburg Music Festival was born, and it succeeded beyond anyone's wildest expectations.

Although, at first, the city fathers expected to attract a few music lovers from neighboring European countries, there are now more Americans, Japanese and even Arab oil sheiks than German and French professors, musicians and students in Salzburg during the festival season. The narrow streets are crowded with Mercedes and other super-expensive cars. In front of the modern festival halls (built when it became evident that the castles would no longer be large enough to hold the crowds) Rolls Royces line up for some of the star-studded musical performances. At as much as $100 per ticket, they sell out long before the festival starts, which is usually in late July.

Some of the charming medieval and renaissance houses have been turned into inns. The music school has expanded, and so has the concert season. Although the great festival halls are only used during July and August, the concerts in the palaces (which now feature heat as well as electricity) go on year round.

But many other cities have not been as creative, or lucky enough to have a major composer as a native son. They were unable to turn themselves into monuments of a glorious past when their situations faded into significance. Many formerly vital and important cities seem to have been content to rest on their laurels, and eventually sometimes to die.

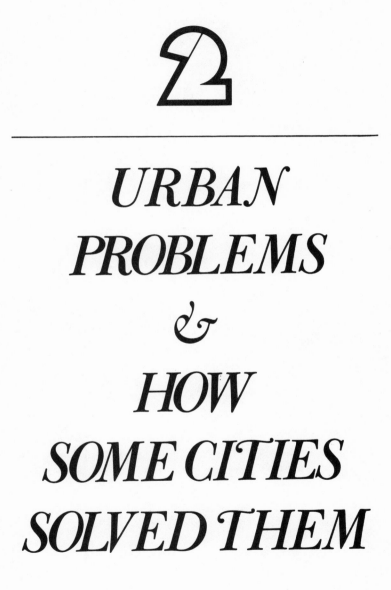

2

URBAN PROBLEMS & HOW SOME CITIES SOLVED THEM

5

Government, Taxation and the Governed

Cities are pestilential to the morals, the health and the liberty of man. . . .

Thomas Jefferson

It's a great place to visit, but I wouldn't want to live here.

Favorite saying among New York visitors

They don't know how to handle money. All they know is how to spend it.

President Ford discussing New York City's financial problems with the somewhat puzzled members of the City Council in Belgrade, Yugoslavia

Give me your tired, your poor,
your huddled masses, yearning to breathe free
The wretched refuse of your teeming shore.
I lift my hand beside the golden door.

Part of a poem by Emma Lazarus, carved at the base of the Statue of Liberty in New York Harbor

If Thomas Jefferson had had his way, Americans might never have built large cities. He argued consistently that the hope of this country lay in its farmers, "the sturdy yeoman," who, in his opinion, were "the true source of the Republic's health." His English ancestors would have agreed with him.

While on the European continent the aristocratic, the wealthy and the cultured were building palaces, universities, churches and parks with fountains in their center cities, the British aristocracy lived on its country estates and equipped its cities with only the most meager necessities. Until the beginning of this century, a British family proved its claim to gentility by living as far away from any large city as possible. Those who governed England journeyed to London for sessions of Parliament and then usually decamped as quickly as possible to their country seats.

Members of the Royal Family might be expected to spend part of their time in London, since that city was, after all, the capital of the Empire, but their generous subjects provided, even for the King and Queen, several tempting country palaces.

British writers and poets frequently shared the anti-city bias of the gentry. "I loathe the squares and streets and the faces that one meets," said Lord Tennyson. "We do not look on our great cities for the best morality," said Jane Austen. Once a hero in a Charles Dicken's novel moves to London, the reader can expect nothing but trouble for him.

Our ancestors brought a great many valuable British ideas to the United States. For instance, British Common Law, with its premise that an accused is innocent until proven guilty, forms the basis of most of our own criminal statutes and court procedures. We got many of our guarantees of freedom from our English forefathers. But we also inherited some of the British prejudice against cities and city dwellers . . . and, in a way, we applied those notions more literally than they were applied in England.

For instance, the British realized very early in their history that, like it or not, it was obviously going to cost a great deal more to run London or Liverpool or Birmingham than an equal number of square miles of orchards, grazing lands and quaint cottages. In Great Britain almost all tax moneys from the entire nation go into a national treasury, which makes funds available to cities according to their needs. Of course, there has never been enough money to support cities as adequately as their citizens have felt they should be supported—but then most country villages have thought that they should be getting more money too.

On the other hand, the British took their anti-city prejudices seriously enough never to trust cities to govern themselves. Parliament and the national treasury have always kept a tight grip on expenses. The Mayor of the City of London (which is actually only a borough in the London metropolitan area) appears in gorgeous traditional robes at the opening of parliament, at royal birthdays and weddings, and at dedications of new monuments in his borough. He makes speeches and cuts ribbons. If he doesn't have a title at the beginning of his term, he's usually knighted when he retires. During his term he is known as The Lord Mayor. But he is not expected to make up a budget for his own borough, never mind the rest of London. He is consulted, of course, as a matter of courtesy, but the actual decisions are made by urban experts in the national government. Since he does not have the responsibility of even a small town mayor in the United States, he doesn't have the power either. London city officials will proudly tell any visitor (especially one from the United States) that there never has been any scandal involving the Mayor's office in *their* city. A tactful visitor will bite his or her tongue and not point out that where there is very little money to spend, there's usually very little graft either.

Many other countries throughout the world have imitated the British system of electing or appointing ceremonial mayors—usually men (and now occasionally women) who have served their cities well in the past as leaders of the business community. The kind of person who might be elected president of the local Chamber of Commerce in the United States receives the title of "Mayor" in those countries that have been influenced by the British system

of government. In other countries mayors and city governments have more power in deciding how funds allocated to
the city by the central government are to be spent. But the
United States is unique in giving city mayors, city councils
and city tax collectors almost total responsibility for governing the city and for raising and spending tax money
as well.

The government of the United States has given those
who run its urban centers enormous power. The Big City
Boss, complete with cigar in his mouth, diamond ring on
his pinky, and a fat gold chain hanging over his bulging
stomach is a uniquely American figure. Sometimes, he is
a mayor who seems to be reelected almost automatically.
Sometimes he is the chairman of whatever political party
has been running the city. And sometimes, he just seems
to be a man who somehow has gathered a great deal of
influence over city government, is able to distribute favors,
and is therefore also able to collect bribes.

"The irrelevant images of small town and rural America were held in common by those who drafted the democratic charters," says Scott Greer, an expert on urban affairs.
"These architects assumed that the farmer, the independent
producer, had both the ability and the interest to govern
himself through the ballot, and through taking public office.
The reality was the mass of new urbanites, employees,
entrepreneurs, hucksters from every part of the earth, often
illiterate, but anxious to make their way in a frightening
and promising environment.

"The result was the invention of the city 'machines'
. . . networks of party clubs which sold favors wholesale
at the top and distributed rewards downward at retail. . . .
the public treasury, the transportation system, the use of
urban lands, the administration of justice . . . all levers
capable of controlling the development of the city . . .
were co-opted by private enterprise. The public purpose
had markedly little to do with the developing layout of
American cities."

Strange as it may seem, the Big Boss often becomes

a kind of folk hero. Everybody knows he is basically crooked . . . but there's something picturesque, or even lovable, about him. Mayors and party chairmen have been allowed to run cities when they were under indictment for all sorts of crimes. Mayor Michael Curley of Boston even ran the city from a jail cell. When he was released, jubilant crowds greeted him at the prison door.

Newspaper accounts of Mayor Curley's release from prison featured the usual man-in-the-street interviews. "Why are you here?" a reporter asked a woman-in-the-street who identified herself as a housewife with seven children. "Because I'm glad the Mayor is out," she said. "Did you feel he was jailed unjustly?" the reporter asked. "Of course not," the woman answered. The reporter apparently didn't pursue his questions any further.

The late Mayor Hague of Jersey City informed the public that *he* was the law. There were few who contradicted him. As a matter of fact, Congressional candidates, and even Presidents, have allowed themselves to be photographed shaking hands with the great man. It took the opposition party to put a few dents in the Mayor's armor. He was finally defeated by a "reform" candidate, whose support came from the city's business community, which realized that the Mayor was no longer useful. A decade later, Jersey City political bosses were again in trouble.

A motion picture, *Chinatown,* recounts in graphic detail the corruption of the city administration in Los Angeles. At a celebration in Los Angeles, attended by hundreds of movie stars and city officials, it received an Academy Award. Nobody took notice of the irony.

Americans expect their cities to be corrupt and unable to govern themselves, either efficiently, or honestly. And yet they have handed over to city government more power than any other country in the world.

City governments are allowed to determine how to tax their citizens and how to spend those taxes. They decide what can be built where, how many cockroaches will be allowed in the city's restaurants, and how many potholes allowed in the city's streets. A local board of education decides who will be educated where, and by whom.

Of course, there are some state and federal regulations that cities have to observe in making vital decisions about the health, welfare and education of its citizens. But "local option" (*i.e.,* leaving almost all governmental functions up to local governing bodies) is an important principle of our system of government.

So, if we distrust our city administrations, why do we continue to allow them such wide choices in the way they govern us? Why do we almost seem to expect corruption in city hall when we would be appalled by similar shady deals and behavior in our state houses or the Halls of Congress? Are there advantages to our system of local self-government, as well as disadvantages? New York is our largest city. Both the problems and advantages of city life and government experienced by other urban centers are magnified there. At the moment New York is in serious trouble. Let's look at some of the causes and results.

Naturally enough, President Ford's assessment of New York City's problems bothered the city's leaders. "I never thought I'd see the day when a President of the United States would go around the world talking disparagingly about any part of this country," former Mayor Abraham Beame plaintively told a *New York Times* reporter. The former President of New York City's Council wasn't just plaintive, he was downright furious. "It amounts to crass stupidity . . .," said Paul O'Dwyer. "There is no point in sending a man across to other countries unless he's a goodwill ambassador. He might just have maintained a diplomatic silence." Apparently, it didn't occur to either of the New York City fathers that the President might actually have said something positive about their troubled community. After all, the loudest applause President Ford received during pre-election speeches throughout the United States was when he promised not to "bail out" New York City.

"As a target, New York City has always been hard to

miss," said *Time* magazine, in reporting on the President's attitude. "It has always been the biggest, sassiest and liveliest city in the country. . . . Not everyone hates the Big Apple, of course. But President Ford's confident assault suggested that New York was awash in coast-to-coast currents of free-floating hostility that suddenly threatened to make it a city without a country."

Nor was the President the only public figure to administer verbal kicks to New York when the city seemed down. "It's an American tradition to cheer when a big guy stumbles," said Governor Daniel Evans of the State of Washington. "And if New York is bailed out, where is the incentive for other people to manage their affairs prudently?" Governor Evans did not mention the fact that the largest city in his state, Seattle, had been in serious trouble only a short while before. Seattle depended heavily on its aircraft industry. And the industry depended on its principal customer: the United States Government. When the United States decided it needed fewer planes and missiles, unemployment in Seattle skyrocketed to the highest point in the city's history. Stores were empty, and many closed. Even banks felt threatened, because homeowners could no longer keep up mortgage payments and defaulted on loans. For a while, people in other cities were actually sending food packages to Seattle, to be distributed free-of-charge to families whose unemployment insurance had run out. Eventually, the United States Government decided it needed more planes and missiles after all, and Seattle business began to hum again as unemployment dropped. Indirectly, of course, some of the funds that helped to "bail out" Seattle came from U.S. taxpayers.

In November of 1975 a Gallup poll showed that 74 percent of the nation's farmers opposed federal aid to New York. Yet farmers, through subsidies and other grants, have always been high on the nation's bail-out list.

"The thing I don't like about New York is a tendency to reward bums and penalize hard work," explained ex-Governor of Georgia, Lester Maddox, while serving fried chicken in his newly integrated restaurant. Formerly he had wielded an ax handle to drive out black customers, but the U.S. government eventually had convinced him that if he wished to stay in business, he would have to admit all fried chicken fans as long as they could pay their bills. While he was governor, members of his staff were frequently quoted as saying that all those who did not enjoy Georgia's racial and economic climate might be supplied with one-way tickets to New York, where welfare payments were more generous. There are probably enough ex-Georgians living in New York to fill a medium-sized southern town.

If New York and other northeastern cities are in financial trouble, one of the reasons may be that, early in our history, the city fathers took the poem on the base of the Statue of Liberty seriously. From the beginning of the nineteenth century to the middle of the twentieth, immigrants from throughout the world, "those huddled masses yearning to breathe free," streamed into New York harbor.

Because so few of the newcomers understood any English, the United States government hired interpreters to work at Castle Garden and later at Ellis Island. One of them on Ellis Island was a young man of partly Italian, partly Jewish heritage, Fiorello La Guardia, who later became a reform mayor of New York City, and one of the best and most respected mayors that city ever had. "I never managed during those years I worked there to become callous to the mental anguish, the disappointment and the despair I witnessed almost daily . . . at best the work was an ordeal," he wrote later in his life.

And yet, new waves of immigrants arrived every day, a few to settle in the Midwest, more in northeastern cities, but the vast majority in New York. They definitely wanted to live there, even though they knew from earlier immigrants that life would continue to be an enormous struggle. And New York City, sometimes reluctantly, accepted those newcomers as it accepted the poor and those who sought new opportunities from every part of the United States.

There was no question about one fact: *the newcomers*

definitely wanted to live in the city, in New York, with all its problems, its slums, and, its incredibly difficult and confusing new life style. New York, to them, presented at least a chance to rise from the bottom of the ladder, to make one's own way in a new world. And for many, New York fulfilled that promise. But for others it did not. And these became the people who went on welfare. Sometimes just for a while, sometimes for a lifetime.

Welfare is not the only source of New York's money problems, of course. There are many political and economic reasons why a city like New York, expected to support itself, can never quite succeed. It simply costs more to run a city than most cities can raise.

City government in the United States may be corrupt, and it may be cumbersome, and perhaps even outmoded. But its problems are not entirely its own problems. They are the problems of the nation being shouldered by the few. And what is true in the United States is true in every nation in the world, except that no other nation expects its cities to be self-supporting.

6

Money

Above all, Wall Street is power. The talk is of stocks, bonds, contracts, bills of lading, of gold certificates and wheat futures, but it is talk that sends fleets steaming to distant oceans, that determines the fate of new African governments, that closes the mining camps in Chibougamou. In the world's great money markets, power has forged massive canyons through which thousands of men and women daily hurry to work, hurry to lunch, hurry, hurry in the shadows of towers tall enough to defy the heavens. Depending on one's point of view, Wall Street is either awesomely impressive or appalling.

No one has ever called it beautiful.

> Emma Latham in *Death Shall Overcome,* a mystery novel in which the detective is a Wall Street banker, John Putnam Thatcher

Shaken homeowners and landlords wobbled out of the county assessors office in Los Angeles last week with rebellion in their eyes. In the suburb of Palos Verdes, Don Johnson, a certified public accountant who earns $25,000 a year, returned dumbstruck to his four-bedroom ranch home. When he and his wife, Ellen Ann, bought the home in 1959, their tax bill was $600 a year. But inflation rates ballooned the assessed value of their home and by last year the Johnson's taxes were $1,593. Last week the taxman released the latest listings. Overnight the assessed value of the Johnson home had soared to $135,000 and the Johnson's taxes threatened to skyrocket to $4,139.

At the assessors office in West Los Angeles, an ashen-faced husband emerged to give similar bad news to his wife, a woman in a matronly blue dress. "Sam, don't tell me," she cried. "I'm going to have a heart attack right here." The uproar over the reassessment was so loud that the assessor, Alexander Pope, hurriedly agreed to a rollback to the county's listings at the 1977 level. But the trauma lingered on.

The Brewing Tax Revolt, Newsweek,
June 5, 1978

Cities run on gas, oil, electricity, tourism, government, business and industry, but most of all they run on money. Money is made in cities, and money is spent in cities. It obviously costs more to run one square mile of downtown London, Paris, New York or even Katmandu than it does to run one square mile of cornfields, pasture land or desert. And since most people are more sensitive on the subject of money than they are on almost any other topic one might think of, the biggest, ugliest and most longstanding arguments between city and country dwellers are usually over finances.

As we noted earlier, in the United States we have the rather unique notion that cities ought to be self-supporting on one hand, but that, on the other, they should send huge amounts of tax money to national and state governments.

All that money in Wall Street that Emma Latham mentions is probably taxed three times: at the federal, state and New York City level. By far the largest percentage of these taxes go to Washington and Albany, the city that for some obscure reason is the capital of the State of New York. (New York City wasn't even in the running when state lawmakers picked a capital city over a century ago.)

Money may be the reason why many of America's largest cities are not the capitals of the state in which they are located. Neither Los Angeles nor San Francisco is the capital of California. Sacramento, a medium-sized town whose only industry is government, is where all that state tax money goes. Ever heard of Montpelier? That's the capital of Vermont, not Burlington. Neither Dallas nor Houston is the capital of Texas, Austin is. So money from large urban centers flows to state capitals, often among the smaller urban communities in the state, and very little of it flows back, since many state legislatures are dominated by representatives from suburban and rural areas who represent constituencies that are singularly uninterested in the fate of large cities: they just don't want their state tax bills raised.

Of course, the lion's share of the tax money raised in our largest cities goes to Washington and becomes a part of the general revenue of the U.S. government. There is in the federal structure a Department of Housing and Urban Affairs, which is supposed to see to it that American cities don't get shortchanged. But the Department has almost as much trouble with the Bureau of the Budget and the U.S. Congress as the Department of Human Services, another part of the federal structure whose interests supposedly lie in making sure that big city residents, especially the poor, don't suffer undue hardship. Most members of the U.S. Congress, like their counterparts in state governments, are also elected from rural and suburban constituencies, and they too tend to talk a great deal more about what cities cost than what cities earn.

So in the United States, we have a system in which real estate taxes, like those in California, are supposed to support most city services. And in some cities, New York, for instance, where real estates taxes have risen to the point that business and industry have decided they can no longer support the cost of doing business, and landlords have decided that they can no longer afford to maintain and rent their buildings, there is also a city income tax and a city sales tax, as well as those real estate taxes.

As a result, you have the strange situation in which people who live and work in New York City pay almost twice as much in a variety of taxes as those who live and work in neighboring Connecticut. New York City and New

York State both levy income taxes on their residents, who pay the same federal income tax as the citizens of Connecticut. But Connecticut has no state income tax and no Connecticut city (most of which are small enough to barely deserve the designation, "city," at all) has a city income tax. There is a state sales tax, and there are real estate taxes. The sales tax is about the same as the one charged by New York State, and less than what is charged by the state plus the additional levy assessed by New York City. Connecticut residents pay real estate taxes, of course, but the assessments (the amount of money the locality expects the real estate owner to pay, which is based on the estimated value of the property) are usually considerably lower than the assessments on comparable property in or near New York City. What's more, the mill rate (that's the percentage of the assessed value that the property owner is supposed to pay in taxes) also tends to be lower.

So what happens is that a resident of Riverdale (a high income section on the outskirts of New York City) may pay as much as 20 percent of his or her income in state and, especially, in city taxes, while a resident of Greenwich, a town just across the Connecticut border, with the same income and with property worth at least as much, pays about 5 percent.

Many experts believe that tax structures like these may be one of the principal reasons so many of our cities are in such serious trouble. When New York City was on the verge of bankruptcy, the problem made headlines all over the world. But no one, except its own residents, took much notice of the fact that Detroit, Cleveland, Newark and any number of other cities in the Northeast and Middle West have even more serious financial crises.

Actually, the same experts who point their fingers at the problems caused by our tax structure and our general dislike of facing city crises, feel that New York City may actually be the *last* financially troubled U.S. urban center to go officially broke. Those Wall Street bankers who, according to Emma Latham, decide the fate of much of the world's population, have lent New York enough money over the years to become seriously concerned when there's talk of legal bankruptcy, which would mean that New York would no longer be obligated to pay all those debts. When a New York City bankruptcy was averted several years ago through a whole series of guaranteed state and federal loans, those bankers and their powerful lobbyists in Washington and Albany probably had as much to do with the actions of the state legislature and the U.S. Congress as all the big city mayors who went to Albany and Washington to lay their rather desperate cases before some highly unsympathetic legislatures.

As long as we insist that cities have to support most of their own services, be it hospital care, education, police and fire protection, the welfare of the poor and all the other special needs of their citizens, we will probably continue to have cities that seem to live from one crisis to the next, with the resulting decay of the cities and the flight of many of their citizens to the suburbs or to the so-called Sunbelt region of the Southwest. There, because cities are still relatively new and growing, many of the problems of the northeastern and middlewestern cities have not occurred . . . yet.

In many parts of the country harassed taxpayers are attempting to stem the tide of rising real estate assessments and mill rates. In California, in 1978, the property owners voted overwhelmingly for a law called, "Proposition 13," which rolled back taxes drastically and eventually slashed seven billion dollars from that state's property taxes. Those who opposed Proposition 13 said that fire and police protection in the cities would have to be cut drastically, that libraries would close, that schools would have to operate on double sessions and that some might have to curtail all extra-curricular activities, that California's extensive free state college system would have to be cut severely, or that tuition rates as high as those in private colleges would have to be charged. None of these predictions came true, but only because the state government in Sacramento had amassed a sizable surplus from taxes of previous years. This surplus was immediately made available to cities and towns in the state to make sure that vital services (especially those affecting the relatively wealthy and the middle class) would not be seriously affected. At first glance, it looked as if all those anti-Proposition 13 prophets had been wrong, but the final bill is not yet in. The surplus is now running out . . . and the cuts that were expected for the late 1970s may actually occur in the early 1980s.

Nor is the financial outlook for cities in other parts of the United States any more promising for the next decade. Indeed, the financial problems of cities are creating a kind of vicious circle. Those residents who can afford to live in the suburbs or the rural areas surrounding cities are doing so in greater and greater numbers. Understandably enough, they would rather not bear the financial burden of keeping our large cities alive and well against overwhelming odds. Many of these large cities therefore are losing population—often the population that can be counted upon to pay the largest share of the tax load. Further, any loss of population brings with it another problem: the loss of votes in state legislatures and the U.S. Congress.

In 1979, it had already become clear that after the figures of the latest census became official, New York City would lose at least four seats in the U.S. Congress. Congress is based, as are all other legislative bodies, on a one-man, one-vote system. This system once worked in favor of cities (indeed, the U.S. Supreme Court decision that set up the principle was based on the opinion that rural and suburban areas were over-represented in legislative bodies and urban areas under-represented). But as people have left cities to settle elsewhere, the composition of the legislatures, on the state and federal level, that will decide on tax policies and on the kinds of subsidies to be offered to cities, will become more and more suburban and rural. And, as we noted earlier, those fine folks out in the country, which is not really country, but an extension of the city, do not want to be taxed in order to solve city problems.

That's why many of them moved away from cities in the first place.

How are cities financed in other countries of the world? Few have the three-part kind of tax system we have in the United States. Most are financed out of allocations from the general tax revenues of the countries in which they are located. But that is not to say these cities are free of financial problems. Their finances are entirely dependent on the relative strength of their country's economy and, in some parts of the world, on the country's ability or willingness to collect income and other kinds of taxes from all its citizens.

There are countries in the world, including some in Western Europe, where cheating the tax collector has become a national pastime. Americans may not like to pay taxes any better than their counterparts in Italy or France, but they pay their taxes with surprising honesty and promptness. In other countries, in which the whole tax system is neither as free from corruption or as eager in its enforcement policies as it is in the United States, taxes simply don't get paid at all, or only a small percentage of what is actually due ever reaches the coffers of the government. In Italy and several other European countries, industrialists, movie stars and others often pay taxes at about the same rate as a worker in a factory or a waitress in a cafe; and when the government catches up with them, the super-rich usually manage to drag court cases into decades of appeals and counter-appeals. Some who are finally ordered by a court to pay the taxes owed quickly follow their money out of the country to such tax havens as Switzerland or Monaco, where they can live in complete safety from their own country's tax collectors.

So, although the system of distributing tax monies for cities may be a lot fairer in other countries than it is in the United States, the system of collecting the taxes is not nearly as fair. And mayors from Rome, Paris and other large cities make the same desperate trek to the legislatures of their countries as the mayors of New York, Detroit and

Cleveland make to Washington. The results of their pleas
are often quite similar, too. They receive a lot of good advice on how to affect savings and how to run their cities
more efficiently, but very little of the hard cash that is
needed to solve their problems.

There are governments that seem to be able to support
cities equitably and well, most notably in the Scandinavian
countries and Switzerland. But these countries are rich by
any standard. They seem to have few serious economic
crises, very few national emergencies, a stable currency
and, most importantly, almost no poverty-stricken minority
populations or segments of citizens who are chronically
unemployed. It's quite interesting to note that neither
Sweden nor Switzerland has been involved in any war for
the past century, and that both countries spend only a
negligible amount on armies and armaments. Historians
point out that this does not necessarily mean that either
Sweden or Switzerland is more peaceful and fair than other
countries in the rest of Europe and the world. It does mean,
however, that for a number of complicated political and
economic reasons, they have been safe from invasion and,
therefore, safe from having their economic systems disrupted by the kinds of huge costs that wars of the past and
preparation for potential wars of the future entail. Much
of the money that was saved in this manner has gone into
vast programs of social improvement, and of course, a sizable percentage of these funds has gone to the cities. So
Stockholm, Zurich and Geneva have almost none of the
urban problems that face almost all other cities in the rest
of the world.

Some cynics maintain that Sweden and Switzerland
are safe because those who make wars keep all their money
there. There is absolutely no evidence that this is so . . .
although the laws of Switzerland, which make it possible
for banks to establish numbered bank accounts (with no
name attached to them), certainly seem like a clear invita-
tion to those who would prefer to have no one know where
their money is and how much they have.

There have been many suggestions on how to solve the money problems that seem to afflict the majority of the world's cities. They have ranged from the totally ridiculous: cut New York off from the mainland and float it out to sea; or make each city a separate state within the United States, so that taxes that normally go to Albany or Montpelier or Sacramento will go to the city, or just let all those impoverished cities stew in their own problems until they die. To the fairly sensible it seems necessary to find a tax structure that will make everyone who lives in a given country responsible for the welfare of its cities, and then collect the taxes that are owed to fulfill the responsibility that has been acknowledged.

But the fact is that cities will continue to have money problems until those who live away from city centers acknowledge that a country needs its great cities to be a country at all. Cities are a necessity, not an expensive luxury. Without them the farmer who grows his corn, the industrialist whose company manufactures everything from toothpicks to supersonic aircraft, the musician who plays his violin, and the writer who wants his work published would probably have nowhere to go to sell whatever he or she does. Even the adamant rural legislator will admit that a country without cities would, in the twentieth century, be an economic, political and social impossibility. If he would just draw the logical conclusion from his admission, half of the financial problems experienced by the cities of the world would be solved. And with their financial problems resolved, everything also might just fall into place. Someone (probably a very rich person) once said that money is the root of all evil. The chances are that the opposite is true: *lack* of money creates many of the world's problems, and certainly lack of money may actually *be* the problem that threatens the existence of some of the greatest cities of the world.

7

Education, Welfare, Health and Other Expensive Problems

Efforts to eradicate illiteracy in United States cities are grossly inadequate and varied approaches are needed to help tens of millions of adults who lack the skills to perform basic tasks, according to a report issued by the Ford Foundation.

New York Times, August 1979

Being a mother is a noble status, right? So why does it change when you put "unwed" or "welfare" in front of it?

Attorney Florence R. Kennedy, quoted in an article in *MS* magazine, 1973

In the United States today, mental health care of high quality and reasonable cost should be readily available to all who need it. This is not the case.

Report of the President's Commission on Mental Health, 1978

Recently, a rehabilitation center in a large New England city received a grant to study why some people, who seemed to have no specific physical problem and who obviously wanted and needed jobs, either could not find work or could not keep it, if they were lucky enough to get it. The center had an excellent record at training and finding employment for people with all kinds of physical handicaps. Jobs also had been found for men and women who had been severely emotionally disturbed, retarded or who had spent time in prisons. Yet there were some adult men and women for whom the center apparently would do very little. They showed up once, pleaded with the counselor to help them find jobs, and then when they were scheduled for aptitude and intelligence tests, simply did not return. The counselors were puzzled by these people. They did not seem to be lazy . . . the impression was that they really wanted to work. Often they seem bright and interesting. So why did they refuse the help that was offered when they had asked for it?

A follow-up on these people provided an answer: almost to a man or a woman, they were illiterate and were desperately embarrassed by that fact, too embarrassed to come for a written examination. Somehow, they had managed to get to adulthood, hiding their inability to read from all but their closest relatives. The counselors came to the conclusion that their illiteracy was the *only* reason they had not been able to find steady jobs. After all, almost any type of work requires a minimal ability to read instructions.

Once the center staff discovered what the difficulty was, they got in touch with their clients and explained that learning to read and write as an adult was not a major problem. A brief literacy course would make it possible for them to learn enough to get and hold a job, which was, after all, what they wanted.

The majority of those reached by staff members returned to the center, took an eight-week course and were placed in permanent jobs. A follow-up study a year later showed that all of these clients had kept their jobs, and that several of them had received raises and promotions.

As part of the program, the counselors did a careful background study of the more than one hundred people involved. They had expected to find that most came from

People

Some come to pray at Jerusalem's Wailing Wall as a daily
ritual.

Above: People are what make a city, more than buildings. These children are on their way to school in Hong Kong.

Above right: In India few schools are coeducational and students usually go sightseeing in groups. Foreigners with cameras generally still attract more attention than ancient ruins.

Below right: Everywhere children love T-shirts, American TV shows and transistor radios. These children in Kyoto, Japan, are no exception.

Above: Children in Istanbul, Turkey, come from many races and ethnic groups. Unlike their elders, they seem to get along with each other exceedingly well.

Right: A London bobby manages to guard a government building without carrying any weapon, not even a nightstick.

Real gurus in India get lots of respect and very little money.

remote rural areas, that they had not attended school and/ or that they were first generation Americans who had never really learned English. The statistics showed almost exactly the opposite to be true. Most had been born and had attended school in the city in which the center was located. All had high school diplomas. None was a first generation American . . . English was the native language of all. All were of average intelligence. So how had they managed to slip through the school system without even an elementary knowledge of reading and writing?

As it turned out, the findings of the Rehabilitation Center fitted into a national pattern. A Ford Foundation report, issued in 1979, stated that 23 million adults in the United States were illiterate and that an additional 34 million could not read and write well enough to pass even the most elementary test. A great many of these individuals had attended schools in urban areas. Some had dropped out, but many had received high school diplomas.

School attendance is compulsory. Most states only allow students to leave after the tenth grade, or at sixteen. Then why are we producing millions of adults who somehow, in some way, have managed to leave urban schools without even the most elementary skills? The answer lies obviously in an educational system that is not geared to helping those who need help the most. Children who attend inner-city schools are most likely to come from families that cannot help their children and sometimes do not even encourage their children to make the most of their school opportunities. As a result, these children need more carefully developed school curriculum and more teachers to challenge and interest them. Yet these are the schools that these days seem to have the least amount of money and personnel.

For centuries, people throughout the world have migrated to cities to make sure that their children received an education. In countries where school is not mandatory, parents still leave the rural countryside and move into cities to assure their youngsters a place in school. Many of the desperately poor city dwellers of the Middle East, South America and Asia will tell anyone who asks that they moved to a city slum in order to get their youngsters into some kind of school, since there was no school available to them in the rural countryside. The same was true, until very recently, in the United States. In cities like New York, Boston, Philadelphia, San Francisco and Chicago, the schools were once considered superior to the one-room schoolhouse in a sparsely populated prairie or mountain area. New York City even provided a free, superb college system for extra-bright high school graduates. Many cities had specialized high schools for those who wished to become scientists, dress designers, or performing artists. Then how was it possible for millions of Americans to get through city schools with no visible signs of education?

One of the reasons for this is again our highly unique system of financing city services. In France, England, Germany, India, Turkey and almost any other country one cares to mention, education is financed, to a large extent, by the national government. Since more people tend to live in cities than in the country, the government spends most of its educational allotment on these cities. A system where each city is responsible for most of the cost of educating its children is almost unique to the United States. The result has been that suburban and, frequently, rural schools are now better than those in central cities. In some cities, the whole educational system has become part of a vicious circle: as schools get worse, because there is less money, more parents move to the suburbs to make sure that their children get an adequate education; as parents move, the tax base shrinks; and as the tax base shrinks, the schools get still worse.

In smaller, better-staffed school systems than the one existing in the New England city where the center was located, the non-readers would probably have been spotted by the third grade and given the kind of remedial instruction they needed to catch up. In the under-financed, under-staffed school system the rehabilitation center clients attended, a youngster could bluff his or her way through twelve years of school without anyone noticing that he or she could not read the inscription on the high school diploma awarded at graduation.

Of course, the vast majority of people in the United States, in cities as well as in the suburbs of country, learn how to read, but it is now generally assumed that schools in inner-city areas are not as good as schools in affluent suburbs. The U.S. Supreme Court recently took note of that fact when the justices found that it was no longer possible to finance schools entirely from local real estate taxes. The decision, made after a group of parents in a New Jersey city sued the state government, held that affluent suburbs could, by the nature of the tax structure, provide a much better education for their children than large, crowded, impoverished cities. School funds would have to be more equally divided, the Court decreed. This has caused all kinds of havoc in state legislatures, which now have been forced to devise methods of financing educations that do not rely entirely on city real estate taxes. In New Jersey, one of the ways has been to legalize casino gambling in Atlantic City. Some of the gambling money is supposed to go to the state to use for improvements in urban school systems. Whether this is going to work or not, nobody as yet knows.

Of course, most schools in the United States receive some money from the federal government, and poorer districts are supposed to get more than richer ones. But this still has not made the amount of money spent on city school children equal to that spent on suburban students. Families still move away from cities to get a better education for their children in suburban or rural school systems. The very rich and the very poor are increasingly the ones remaining in the center cities. The rich send their children to private schools, and the poor have to make do with what is available to them. Meanwhile, the quality of education in many American cities declines. Some cities that have actually gone bankrupt—Cleveland, for instance—or that are on the verge of bankruptcy have had to shorten the school year, or have threatened to close schools altogether. Obviously, this state of affairs cannot be allowed to continue indefinitely. Someone will have to come up with a plan to improve city schools so that everyone will have at least a chance to get a better education than is now being received by city children.

In other parts of the world, the financing problem may be difficult, but cities are still having to struggle to meet the needs of millions of children who want and need an education. In some of the less developed countries, the vast majority of youngsters still don't get any schooling at all. But slowly, some of this is changing. Even when the laws don't require children to go to school, families are becoming more and more aware of one indisputable fact: to break out of poverty, schooling is the one essential ingredient. All over the world, more children go to school with every passing year. And since transportation in many of those countries is still very limited, most of the schools are built in urban areas. There are usually a few rural elementary schools, but any type of higher education is available only in large cities. The government may provide some kind of dormitory space for children who come to the cities so that the whole family does not have to leave the farm in order to make it possible for youngsters to go to school beyond the fourth grade.

Increasingly, countries, especially some of the developing ones, are also providing vocational high schools, junior colleges, and even universities for their young people. Some of the money earned by the oil rich countries like Saudi Arabia is being invested in higher education for those who can qualify. Many of these nations are realizing that no natural resources, not even the highly prized petroleum, will, in the long run, provide security. After all, oil will eventually run out, and before that, some of the industrial nations may have found alternative sources of energy. So, to secure their futures, they must have technically trained experts—and importing these experts, as they export their oil, does not seem like a permanent solution.

Thus as the oil rich cities grow, so do their government-sponsored education programs.

Ironically, America, which pioneered universal education and had one of the best public school systems in the world for many generations, seems to be putting less emphasis on education, especially city schools, while other, less-developed countries are devoting more of their money to education.

America is also unique in expecting its cities to pay for other human services. Most Western European countries, as well as Canada, provide family grants to mothers with dependent children, regardless of financial need. In the United States, the federal government provides some welfare funds to the very poor, but much of the cost of welfare is again borne by the cities in which these families live. One program, A.D.C. or Aid to Dependent Children, is funded on three levels: federal, state and local. And the local allocation, which has to be financed through city property taxes, and occasionally, as in New York City, through city income and sales taxes as well, takes a considerable bite out of the overall budget of cities. Everywhere in the world, the poor have traditionally moved to cities. But almost nowhere in the world, except in the United States, are the cities expected to bear the principal cost of keeping these families from complete destitution. Every candidate of every political party promises cities that "something" will be done to relieve the local treasury of at least some of these welfare costs. Yet, in the past few decades little has been done. The vast majority of those who receive welfare checks are small children, their mothers who must care for them, the elderly and the disabled. Yet, everywhere in the United States, there is an impression that the welfare system is loaded down with healthy, adult loafers, living it up at the taxpayers' expense.

Almost every big city mayor knows that there really is no way to cut welfare costs, and almost no rural legislator believes that this is true. Of course, as welfare costs rise with the cost of living, less money is available for education in American cities, and more of those able to pay taxes and who don't need the various costly city services the poor require move out. This is one problem that will have to be solved soon, unless we wish more American cities to follow the example of Cleveland. That city went bankrupt twice within one year . . . partly because the city treasury could no longer support the increased costs of welfare and education.

Add to these two problems the expense of providing health and mental health services. Not so long ago, most American cities were able to provide some health care through city-owned and operated hospitals. But as the costs of medical care have risen, cities have attempted to close these hospitals and to buy medical care for their neediest citizens from private, non-profit care facilities. This too has become increasingly expensive.

Our health care funds, like those of education and welfare, come from three sources: local, state and federal, and the same educational formula that keeps cities broke applies to health dollars as well. The old, the physically and mentally ill, the teen-age, unwed mother and her baby are concentrated in our cities—and the cost of giving these people even minimally adequate care is another serious drain on city treasuries.

Health care in the United States, especially in our major cities, can be the best in the world for those who can afford to pay: either because they are able to manage the high costs out of income or because they have insurance. But medical care for the poor is often abysmal. We still have one of the highest infant mortality rates in the civilized world, and many of the babies who die during their first month of life are born to poor inner-city mothers who have little or no prenatal care, little education and few opportunities to escape poverty.

In most other Western countries, there is some form of national health insurance in which everyone participates and from which everyone benefits. There are, of course, innumerable arguments as to whether the care provided through this system is as good as American health care *at its best,* but no one doubts that the kind of care provided in Stockholm or Amsterdam, or even Rome, to the poorest citizens is better than the care provided to the very poor in most of America's large cities. And again, the cost of even this minimal care is another severe drain on city budgets. When big city mayors tell their constituents that they will have to "tighten their belts" in the area of health care, they don't mean that most people will not be able to get medical help when we need it. What they mean is that health care for the poor will be cut further. In New York City in 1979, the mayor planned to close two hospitals, which saw more than three hundred and fifty thousand people a year in their outpatient clinics alone, because of the budget crunch. At the same time, in those same areas, schools were also being closed, so class sizes increased and the number of teachers decreased. The city budget was still deeply in the red, and a real solution to the educational, welfare and health problems in the city, and in most other cities, was nowhere in sight.

8

Filth

Pollute: to make impure, soil, defile . . . pollution, noun.

> The New American Webster's Handy College dictionary

. . . the gully pits could not be cleared because the inlets were choked, the inlets could not be cleared because the manholes were choked, the manholes could not be cleared because the sewers were choked, and the sewers could not be cleared because the pumping stations were weak . . .

> A communication received in India by the Calcutta Metropolitan Development Association from the Calcutta Sanitation Department when the Association asked that some of the worst filth in the streets be cleaned, since an outbreak of cholera was feared in that Indian city

Making her way carefully over the cobblestones, Rosa came to an open cement drain which carried sewage to the beach and the sea. A half-inch pipe, pierced with holes for flushing the sewage lay in the center of the drain, but this primitive system of sanitation was no longer functioning. Garbage, empty cans, old newspapers, a ragged pair of child's panties littered the dry drain.

> A description of La Esmeralda, a shanty town in the center of San Juan, Puerto Rico, in *La Vida* by Oscar Lewis

"Pollution," as applied to filthy streets, water and air is a word that didn't appear in popular books about cities until around 1950. The whole idea of ecology is also relatively new. Until the beginning of the twentieth century, cities were expected to be dirty.

According to author Katie Kelly, who wrote a funny and shocking book called *Garbage: The History and Future of Garbage in America,* the first litterbug was probably Eve. "Although there is little proof of it, it is doubtful that she—given her panicky and probably paranoid state of mind at the time—ate the entire apple," Ms. Kelly says. "Hence, once the fateful bite was taken, it is safe to assume that Eve tossed her unfinished apple to the ground and went on to other things.

"It is generally conceded by historical garbage experts (there are few of them, so academic dissension on these points is rare, if not nonexistent) that Eve's natural reac- tion—the tossing away of the apple—was probably the order of the day for decades, centuries, eons, and ages," Ms. Kelly goes on to speculate. Indeed it was, although the kind of garbage that our ancestors piled up was probably somewhat different from the variety that gives the Sanita- tion Departments of New York, London, Moscow and Shanghai their constant problems today. Our ancestors didn't throw many waste materials away. Anything that couldn't be eaten was used to make clothing, shelter, cook- ing containers, weapons or other useful items.

Not until the fifth century B.C. do we have a record of a garbage dump. In Greece, where life was more civil- ized than in the rest of the Western world, the citizens be- gan to produce refuse. So the Greeks organized troops of slaves to remove unslightly garbage to the outskirts of town. In Crete, they even used human and animal waste to start compost pits.

The first organized garbage brigade, paid for by pub- lic funds, made its appointed rounds in ancient Rome. To quote Ms. Kelly again: "A wagon, pulled by a horse, was accompanied by the world's first sanitation men, wearing togas. As usual, the streets were the logical recepticals for garbage and . . . since neither paper bags nor plastic disposal bags had yet been invented . . . garbage was tossed in its original condition (loose) into the streets. Legions of Roman sanitation men picked their way down the various vias, scooping the stuff into their wagons. From time to time, certain centrally located spots would catch someone's eye, and handy neighborhood dumps would be created. . . . Then, as today, they were unsightly and smelly. Hence, ancient Rome was often emblazoned with signs reading: 'Take your refuse farther out or you will be fined,' complete with arrows pointing away from town." One presumes that the signs were neatly carved in stone, or modern archeologists would not know about them, since even the finest papyrus, the writing material of ancient Romans, was biodegradable.

The Romans are celebrated by those who do research in garbage history not just for their town dumps, but also for their water systems. The Caesars, including the best and the worst, vied with each other to build aquaducts that would carry fresh, clean water from the mountains into the towns. However, there were no similar structures to carry dirty water, along with human waste and other liquid polluting materials, out of town. There are early references to the foul smells of Rome, especially during the hot months, when all those who could afford to do so fled the city for the cleaner air of the countryside.

There were no laws about the disposal of animal and gladiator bodies after the deadly games in the Colosseum, for instance. In a particularly busy Roman week, there might be thousands of such bodies piled behind the Colosseum structure waiting for carts to carry them to open pits on the outskirts of town. As a result of this practice, a large number of altars were dedicated to the Goddess of Fever, and plagues of filth-borne diseases hit the city about once every five years. The rulers tended to blame these misfortunes on unpopular minorities (just as other rulers blamed disastrous city-wide fires on "enemies within"). So a plague could lead to the slaughter of more men, women, children and animals in the Colosseum . . . more unburied bodies on the landscape, and a worsened epidemic of virulent disease.

Sanitation didn't get better during the Middle Ages or the Renaissance either. In fact, it got worse. Mountains of refuse, filth and human and animal waste collected in streets, gutters, ditches and open fields. The castles of Europe were probably filthy, stinking cesspools. Camelot, or its equivalent, looked nothing like the pictures in our favorite books or the scenery provided by the latest Hollywood spectacle. There was no central heat and anything that could be burned on a cold day probably was. The fires in those huge stone fireplaces were anything but fragrant. If there were rich tapestries on the walls, there were certainly no rugs on the floors. Most castles used straw and rushes to cover the cold stone floors. The covering was changed only when the stench and filth from the refuse tossed to the floors became unbearable; then the used covering was dumped outside the castle to mix with the town's garbage. There were, of course, millions of rats and other rodents in the Medieval and Rennaisance cities, and they brought with them every filth-borne disease known to man.

Not until the sixteenth century did the city fathers of London produce a law that stated: "No man shall bury any dung within the liberties of the city."

One historian points out that the Palace of Versailles, constructed in the seventeenth century as the most luxurious and opulent residence built for any king in history, smelled so bad that men and women started using perfumes to cover the obnoxious odors eminating from those splendid halls.

While Westerners, even wealthy and aristocratic ones, lived in comparative squalor, Easterners, from the early Middle Ages, prized private and public cleanliness. In Japan, for instance, streets have been systematically cleaned since the beginning of recorded history. Bathing was regarded almost as a religious ritual. There are countless references in old Japanese documents to "smelly, filthy, round-eyed barbarians." This description did not apply just to the merchant seamen who sailed into Japanese harbors, but to European and American diplomats, missionaries and rich tourists, who would have been appalled by the impression they were creating. Fortunately, few spoke or understood Japanese, and those Easterners who spoke Western languages were brought up in a code of politeness that did not permit them to remark on others' disgusting lack of personal hygiene.

Even today, Japanese cities, which are among the most crowded on earth, are also the cleanest. There are no signs warning citizens not to litter—it's simply not done. A small child who drops a candy wrapper on the ground in a park is asked, firmly and politely, to pick it up. Even in zoos, countless men and women with brooms and shovels clean up after the animals all day long. A New York City law, passed in 1978, that attempts to force dog owners to clean up after their dogs, has existed in Japanese cities for as long as anyone can remember, even though most Japanese don't understand the need for such a law. After all, who would let an animal foul the public street in the first place? Only a barbarian.

To get back to Renaissance Europe, another historian interested in city sanitation indicates that cities got filthier through the centuries, to reach a peak of unbearable pollution probably at the beginning of the nineteenth century. Lewis Mumford, in his book, *The City in History,* says: "In all probability, the early Medieval village or town enjoyed healthier conditions, for all of the crudeness of sanitary accommodations inside and outside the house, than its more prosperous sixteenth century successor. Not only was the town behind the wall sufficiently small to have quick access to open land, but a good part of the population had private gardens behind their houses and practiced rural occupations within the city, just as they did in the typical American small town up to 1890. . . ."

Mumford points out that we don't know very much

about the incidence of infectious diseases in Medieval times. We do know, however, that whole populations were wiped out periodically, probably by germs and viruses that remained unrecognized until our day. But, he maintains, there were also repeated attacks of typhoid and cholera in American and European towns early in the nineteenth century, and as late as 1918, an influenza epidemic killed hundreds of thousands in Western Europe. Mumford also adds that one of the reasons all of Europe was not altogether depopulated by various filth-borne diseases might be the prevalence of fires. If too much filth accumulated, fires broke out, which tended to burn the garbage heaps, along with the wooden houses alongside of them. "Fire is a powerful disinfectant," Mumford says. Apparently the citizens of those plague-prone cities agreed with him. An Elizabethan writer, John Stow, noted that the custom of lighting bonfires during summer festivals did not merely mark a joyous outburst of feeling that winter was over or that the prospects for a good harvest or profitable trade looked promising, but proved "the virtue of a great fire bath to purge infection of the air."

As cities grew, industrial wastes were added to private filth and garbage. "By the 1800s, garbage and growth were inexorably linked," says Katie Kelly. "The Siamese twins of society, garbage and growth, where would one be without the other?" All kinds of attempts were made to keep at least the main city thoroughfares clean. In 1792, when Philadelphia's population was under one hundred thousand, good citizens volunteered their slaves' services to carry loads of garbage on their heads to the Delaware River and to dump them downstream from the city. Charleston, West Virginia, passed a law protecting vultures from being shot "or otherwise killed" by its citizens, since the birds helped to clear some of the worst filth from the streets. Of course, rats ran rampant through the cities. According to one urban historian, New York finally appropriated funds for rat control when, in 1860, a newborn baby was killed by the rodents in its crib at Bellevue Hospital.

By 1890, Washington, D.C. had hired a regular garbage disposal force and acquired some barges to ship the junk and filth that was picked up once every two weeks down the Potomic River toward Alexandria, Virginia. The citizens of that town were understandably not very enthusiastic about the invasion of garbage barges from the north. A regular war ensued: the Alexandrians overturned the barges and sank a few; the Washingtonians bought new barges and sent them out with armed guards.

Eventually, it became evident that the space to be used for dumps was becoming scarce. Someone decided to return to the practice of ancient times: burning the stuff on the outskirts of cities. The first incinerator (called "crematory") was built in England. America followed suit in 1885, and Germany in 1896. We have been burning garbage ever since, but now have started to worry that, as pollutants burn on the ground, the air into which we release the smoke is becoming dirtier with every passing year. The incidence of filth-borne diseases has decreased through the world, but lung cancer rates are growing.

In most cities, crowding, poverty and filth go together. Calcutta, India, is probably the worst example. There, whole sections of the city seem to be drowning in a sea of garbage, human waste and animal droppings. The sacred cows wander through the streets leaving tons of waste behind them. Streets would be totally impassible if cow dung were not prized by some Indians for fuel and, therefore, picked up by men, women and children and carried to huts and hovels in baskets or sacks.

Some of the broadest avenues in Calcutta are periodically cleaned by sweepers. But sanitation equipment is ancient or nonexistent. Even a small army of men and women, who attempt to clean up those parts of town every evening where the rich live and tourists are apt to visit, can hardly make a dent in the mountains of filth. In Calcutta, and in many other large cities, the concept of pollution is still irrelevant. Conditions are so bad that one still has to think about the kind of basic sanitation that concerned our Medieval forefathers.

In recent years, as populations have grown and usable land became scarcer, inventive city planners have begun using collected garbage and trash as land fill. Whole new areas have been built on refuse collected from center cities. At the present time scientists are even experimenting with garbage as a new source of energy. Perhaps the stuff can be burned and the heat it produces used to fuel electric plants. In that way, we might be able to have our garbage and use it, too. But garbage still makes for more problems than benefits.

Within the last ten years, the increasing amount of refuse and waste polluting our landscape, rivers and even our oceans has become a serious concern to another new breed of scientist: the ecologist. What are we doing to our world when we pollute the air with the smoky residue of industrial waste?, they ask. What are we doing to our earth when we fill in wetlands with garbage and build tract housing or airports on this newly created real estate? What is happening to our water when we pump untreated sewage into our rivers and lakes? One ecologist noted that garbage was now floating in the middle of the Atlantic Ocean, somewhere between the new and the old world.

Garbage, or more accurately, the removal of garbage and waste, has become a political issue. Woe betide the mayor who allows trash to accumulate in neighborhood streets. He will soon find a picket line around city hall, whether his offices are located in New York, Paris or West Berlin. The topic that apparently interested the mayor of Paris when the mayor of New York payed him a visit in 1978 was New York City's law requiring dog owners to pick up after their pets. That was exactly what Paris needed, the French mayor said. But how to persuade the Parisian pet owners to carry dog litter bags? "Parisians are individualists," he confided to his New York counterpart. "They don't like stepping into dog droppings anymore than the Americans . . . but it's very hard to persuade them to change their ways."

To date, no one has come up with an answer to the problem of the world's cities drowning in their own waste. Some want to recycle the junk, some bury it, some burn it —but, while we produce more goods, we also produce more junk. As one embattled big city mayor put it recently: "Anyone who finds a way of getting us out from under our piles of garbage should probably win a Nobel Prize." "A Nobel Prize for what?," a reporter asked. "I don't care," the mayor said. "But personally, I'd just give him one for Peace. Perhaps my phone would stop ringing at two A.M. and I'd get a peaceful night's sleep at last."

9

Fire

What ye cannot quench pull down,
Spoil a house to save a town.

> Seventeenth century British poet,
> Robert Herrick, who grew up in a
> London slum called Cheapside, and
> who probably saw the great London
> fire of 1666

We had this fire down the block. A Puerto Rican social club. The captain, the lieutenant and other firemen took the ladder up and saved two people. But downstairs there was a guy trying to get out the door. He was burnt dead. Know what the lieutenant said?: "We lost a guy, we lost a guy." I said: "You save two people. How would you know at six in the morning a guy's in the social club sleeping on a pool table?" He said: "Yeah, but we lost a guy." And the lieutenant is a conservative guy. . . .

There's a saying in the firehouse: "Tonight could be the night." But nobody thinks of dying. You can't take it seriously, because you'd get sick. We have had some fires. I said: "We're not going to get out of this." Like I say, everybody dies.

> Chicago Fireman Tom Patrick, as
> quoted in Studs Turkel's *Working*

Fires are one of the most serious dangers to cities. Many times in the history of the world whole cities have been destroyed by flames, through carelessness, natural disasters and wars. God is said to have rained down fire on the Biblical cities of Sodom and Gomorrah. Troy was destroyed after the Greeks won the city. Nero probably didn't fiddle while Rome was burning, but Rome burned. Many historians think now that he was away in his suburban villa and had the fire set in order to blame it on the Christians, whom he considered a danger to his rule. After the fire hundreds of Christians were killed in Rome's Coliseum as "retribution."

Most city-wide conflagrations have been, of course, accidents. But often the people of a burned-out city, trying to find someone on whom to blame their collective misfortune, have found a scapegoat. For instance, the worst fire experienced by any city in the seventeenth century, the great fire of London, was blamed on "Papists" (Roman Catholics) and the French. No one was formally arrested or tried for setting the fire, but a few known Catholics were lynched in its aftermath.

The fire actually started in the ovens of the King's baker, John Farynor. Samuel Pepys, whose *Diary* gives one of the best pictures of London city life in the last half of the seventeenth century, described the beginning of the fire as seen from his house near the Tower at 3 A.M. on September 2, 1666: "It has started in Pudding Lane near London Bridge and, at first, looked like a minor incident, but, in a high wind, it spread rapidly and eventually engulfed almost all of the inner city."

A wind that blew in from the northeast carried live sparks to the half-timbered houses on both sides of the Thames River. London Bridge burned, and getting to the river to obtain water became increasingly difficult. Besides there really was no good way to carry water to the fire. The streets were too narrow for horse-drawn carriages. Eventually, those who could, fled, and watched their homes, places of business, public buildings and churches go up in flames. The record shows that the fire consumed 89 churches and 13,200 houses along 400 streets. Among the buildings that burned to the ground were Shakespeare's Globe Theater, the Guildhall and the Royal Exchange. Finally,

James, the Duke of York, was put in command of the army and navy, which put out the fire after four days. A rainstorm helped . . . if the weather had not changed, the city might have been destroyed completely.

London was rebuilt and became, in the eighteenth century, one of the world's most modern cities. It took almost two hundred years, and another large fire in 1833, however, to prompt the founding of a formal organization for fire protection. Even then, the insurance companies, not the city fathers, started the first fire brigade. Not until 1861 (after another disastrous fire) did London decide to finance a city-wide fire department with about eighty full-time professional fire fighters.

The great fire of Chicago, on October 8, 1871, developed in a manner that was very similar to the London fire of 1666. A small conflagration, starting in a wood house in the middle of a crowded street, got out of control quickly and eventually consumed an area of over two thousand acres, with eighteen thousand buildings. At least three hundred people lost their lives (by then the city government counted human losses, as well as material ones), and ninety thousand people were left homeless. The fire was eventually put out with the help of soldiers and because a rainstorm wetted down the landscape, which had been tinder-dry because of a drought. No one ever knew exactly who or what started the fire. Popular legend tells us that it began when Mrs. O'Leary's cow kicked over a kerosene lamp in her stable. This story is probably untrue, since the fire started in a section of Chicago where neither Mrs. O'Leary nor anybody else kept farm animals.

Much of San Francisco burned down in 1900; the cause of that fire was unmistakable: an earthquake. Almost the entire central city was destroyed, and again the city's fire fighting ability was not up to the challenge. But San Francisco, like London and Chicago, was rebuilt; this time with earthquake-proof and fireproof buildings and an adequate fire department to protect life and property. The San Francisco earthquake and fire, incidentally, were the in-

spiration for a new kind of motion picture: the disaster
film. The movie, *San Francisco,* is the granddaddy of all
those epics that feature conflagrations, bombings, mass
drownings, giant man-eating sharks and other picturesque
forms of death and destruction.

The fire saved San Francisco from some of the worst
effects of the American depression, which started in 1929.
While other American cities stagnated, San Francisco was
still undergoing a building boom, fueled partly by the need
to rebuild much of its center and partly by the general west-
ward movement of America's population. San Francisco
was one of the few cities that went from the real estate boom
of the 1920s right into the industrial boom of wartime
America in the 1940s, with hardly a period of economic
hardship in between.

When one looks at the kind of fire protection available
to cities before the invention of the gasoline-powered motor,
it's amazing that more cities did not burn down. Usually,
the only way to get water from a river or a lake was to
form a "bucket brigade" with men passing the water along,
with the last person in line pouring it on the flames. Obviously, this did not work too well during a high wind. What's
more, it was exceedingly dangerous for the fire fighters,
especially those closest to the flames. Nor were the bucket
brigades professional paid fire fighters. They were usually
volunteers, recruited quickly from the community once the
fire looked to be serious enough to require more help than
cound be summoned from the family and next-door neighbors.

When fires got out of hand, the army or the navy was
often called, in a last ditch effort to save a city. But most
frequently, the city fathers had to count on nature, a rainstorm or a change in wind direction, to put out a city-wide
conflagration. A few cities experimented with horse-drawn
fire engines (usually after at least one disastrous fire had
already occurred), but inner city streets were narrow, and
even if such equipment was available, it was often impossible to get it through to the source of the fire.

To make the situation even more dangerous, there were few building codes to minimize fire hazards in the major cities of the world until the end of the nineteenth century. Chicago, for instance, waited until the great fire had taken its toll to pass regulations establishing definite standards to make buildings fire resistant.

Now, of course, all that has changed. All over the world fire companies are made up of highly trained, professional firefighters who use sophisticated equipment to help them do the best possible job. Every city in America and Europe has hundreds of regulations to prevent the construction of buildings that constitute fire hazards. Few people now complain of not enough rules and regulations; architects, contractors and city fathers tend to think there are too many. With all the well-trained men, expensive equipment (one fire truck can cost up to one hundred thousand dollars) and air-tight building codes, one might think that burning cities were a historical curiosity, along with horse-drawn carriages and community water wells. Unfortunately, they are not, especially in the United States. Anyone looking out a window as a train pulls into a large American city, may see whole areas of burned-out, blackened tenements. In New York, Chicago, Detroit and St. Louis, there are miles of streets on which only abandoned cats and dogs live in the hulks of buildings that once housed thousands of families.

We now have the technology to fight fires quickly and effectively. There certainly has not been a conflagration similar to the great London or Chicago fires in this century. But along with our ability to master fires, a few of us have, apparently, lost the fear that our ancestors shared as they watched whole cities go up in flames.

The most rapidly growing urban crime is arson: the deliberate setting of fires for revenge, profit, or for no apparent reason at all. In almost any city in the United States, the police and fire departments tell of innumerable serious fires that have been deliberately started to collect insurance, to get back at an employer, a landlord, even a rival in love, or just for a thrill. In New York recently, one young man hurled a can of flaming gasoline into the doorway of a social club because he was angry with a former girl friend who had gone there with another man. The whole building burned down and more than a dozen people were killed or injured. In St. Louis, a public housing project, with apartments for more than ten thousand families, built within the last twenty-five years, had to be closed down and wrecked because small fires were set daily in elevator shafts, corridors and vacant apartments. These threatened the lives of all the residents. The police and the fire departments were helpless to stop these continuing acts of arson, and tearing down the whole project became the only possible solution, in spite of the fact that St. Louis, like many other American cities, has a drastic shortage of low-cost family housing.

Every day, in one large city or another, there are court cases against property owners who have apparently attempted to solve their financial problems by burning down unprofitable buildings to collect insurance. According to the U.S. Department of Justice, organized crime hires out "torches" to set fires for a fee.

Fires may no longer consume whole cities in a day, but instead they destroy them slowly, building by building. Once a building in a deteriorated block burns, the others become harder to rent. And eventually, they may also burn. A burned-out block is a danger to the neighboring blocks. The fear of fire drives families from their flats and their streets. In 1978, when President Jimmy Carter saw the empty and flame-blackened streets of New York's South Bronx, he was appalled. He ordered a pre-development plan for the area and wanted it submitted within months. The plan is still on the drawing boards because, among other difficulties, the New York Fire Department and the Federal Department of Housing and Urban Affairs have not yet solved the problem of how to keep fires from being set once the old buildings are torn down and new construction has been started.

Destruction by arson is still mainly an American problem. Short of urban guerrilla war, European, South American, Asian and African cities seem to be relatively safe from arson for profit or what seems to some American police chiefs to be arson for entertainment. But like all American habits and problems, this particular form of urban blight shows some signs of spreading to the rest of the world. Irish Republican Army members, in 1977, threw fire bombs into fashionable London restaurants. In Germany, urban terrorists have set fires in factories and large industrial buildings in protest of whatever they were protesting that week. Pubs in Belfast and Londonderry were fire bombed regularly by Catholic or Protestant extremists in the late 1970s. But the burning of whole city blocks, for no apparent reason, is still confined to urban areas in the United States. Perhaps Europeans and Asians, who have seen fires consume their cities in wars, are leery of allowing them to burn down in peacetime; when they see the South Bronx in New York from a car or a train window, they often shake their heads in disbelief. Why would anyone want to cause this kind of damage to his own city? a businessman visiting New York from his home in Japan's Hiroshima (burned to the ground in the first atom bomb attack in history), asked. How could the government allow this? In Rome, Naples, Rotterdam and other European cities, there are still burned-out buildings from World War II that the government has not yet managed to tear down and replace. The residents of these cities, visiting New York, or Chicago or St. Louis, understandably wonder why a city untouched by war can look like a bombed-out wasteland.

Most of us are not directly affected by the destruction of parts of our inner cities. The fires don't reach where we live. There are some side effects, of course. No one pays real estate taxes in a burned-out neighborhood, for instance, and so all our taxes go up. If the fire department is busy fighting a huge man-made blaze in one section of town, there are fewer fire fighters available to our own neighborhoods, should a fire break out there.

But Mrs. Jiminez Perez, living with five children under

ten on the top floor of the only building left standing in one block on a formerly busy street in the South Bronx, feels the effect of arson much more directly. She hasn't slept a night in weeks. She's taking pills prescribed by the neighborhood mental health clinic to control her terror. She is sure that eventually someone will set fire to her home . . . and that there is nothing she can do about it. "They won't let me move because there's no place to go," she says of her social worker who has visited repeatedly in answer to her frantic calls and those of the mental health worker who sees her once a week and worries about a possible nervous breakdown. "They say my apartment is still 'habitable.' I'd like to see one of them live here. Sometimes I'm tempted to burn the place down myself . . . so at least we could get out."

10

Crowding

Today it is estimated that 15 million children die each year of malnutrition and related diseases. As James Grant, President of the Overseas Development Council, has put it: "That is the statistical equivalent of detonating, among the children of the world, a Hiroshima-type bomb every three days, every month of the year."

> James J. Gilligan, Administrator of the Agency for International Development (A.I.D.), in a speech, October 26, 1978

Calcutta, it is said, is dying ever since it was built 286 years ago. Disease has struck with different intensity almost all urban settlements . . . Tokyo, Bombay, Jakarta, Cairo, London, Havana, New York, Lima et al. . . .

What remains unknown is whether such cities with their sprawling shanty towns and slums, doubling every six years like some monstrous amoeba, can offer citizens a bearable existence.

> Peter Wilsher and Rosemary Righter, in *The Exploding Cities,* published in New Delhi, India in 1975

. . . in the case of rats, reproduction stops automatically when a certain state of overcrowding is reached, while man, as yet, has no workable system for preventing the so-called population explosion.

> Konrad Lorenz, in *On Aggression*

Konrad Lorenz, one of the world's great researchers into animal behavior, obviously loves all living things, with one exception: rats. He finds rats utterly despicable by any standard of decency. And yet, he finds that humans act, in many ways, more like rats than any other species. Only rats and humans participate in wars. Only rats and humans routinely gang up on the strangers of their own species and tear them to pieces. Rats will slowly and horribly dismember a foreign rat that has had the misfortune to wander into the territory of another rat pack. Rats also organize so that a stronger group within the pack can tyrannically rule a weaker group. But rats have one advantage over people, which Lorenz fears may allow these vicious animals to outlast humans in the scheme of things: they stop breeding when the area in which they live becomes so crowded that there is an insufficient supply of food, water and space for the pack. Humans have not learned to do this.

Other scientists have placed their bets on cockroaches as the species that will outlast humans on this overcrowded earth. Cockroaches, like rats, can eat almost anything, will fight for survival in any environment . . . and stop breeding when their habitat becomes too overcrowded with other cockroaches. Rats and cockroaches have one other fact of life in common with humans: they tend to congregate in cities, especially overcrowded and dirty cities. As the world's cities become more overcrowded, and therefore dirtier, humanity will suffer, but rats and cockroaches will thrive. Even at the height of their animal prosperity, they will know enough instinctively not to increase their numbers to the point where their existence becomes endangered. In that way, they behave more intelligently than the human race, some scientists say.

Let's look at some predictions: John J. Gilligan, former Governor of Ohio and an administrator of one of our most important foreign aid programs, says, "By the year 2,000 more than 600 million people will live in abject poverty on this earth. Most of them will be living in cities." If that doesn't seem dire enough, Administrator Gilligan has a few more statistics to darken the horizon: "Today it is estimated that 15 million children die each year of malnutrition and related diseases. That is the statistical equivalent of detonating, among the children of the world, a Hiroshima-type bomb every three days, every month of the year."

And what happens to the children who manage to survive? Gilligan doesn't see a bright future for many of them either. "In crowded cities in the third world, children are abandoned on the streets because their parents can no longer cope with the burden of feeding and clothing them," he says. It is estimated, for instance, that in Venezuela . . . one of the richer of the developing countries . . . *half of all children in the country have been abandoned.*

The solution that Gilligan suggests is increased aid to these countries to help their people practice population control, as well as assistance with the kinds of agricultural projects that will persuade some of the new city families to return to the land where they can grow food for themselves and for those who have remained in the urban areas. He points out that the more prosperous a country becomes, the lower the birthrate drops. If a family feels that only one or two of its children will survive, they will have ten or twelve to make sure that some are left to care for the parents in their old age. "If they can be sure that the majority of their offspring will grow into healthy adulthood, they are much more apt to accept the kind of birth control programs that are the only way to defuse the population bomb," he says.

He also hopes that in some of these countries, laws will be changed to allow families to own plots of land large enough to enable them to feed themselves and their children. "In many of these developing countries, much of the land is owned by absentee landlords who may not even live in the district," he says. "The small farmers rent a tiny piece of land from the landowner. If they are especially capable, they may eventually be able to save enough money to buy a few hundred square meters. But even this kind of minimal land ownership doesn't provide enough space to grow the food needed to keep a large family from starvation. So, they gravitate to the cities where there often is no work, no shelter, and where the family can survive only on the lowest kind of day labor, if that . . ."

There are whole families who sleep, eat, bear children and die on two square yards of sidewalk and gutter in Calcutta. There are families living in excavated tombs on the outskirts of Cairo, who consider themselves lucky to have such a shelter. Others just live in temporary hovels. In Naples, there are still families living in buildings bombed out during World War II, or in the caves that can be found in the hills surrounding the city.

Occasionally, the migration to the cities is reversed, but only if opportunities in the country seem to promise a better life. In Puerto Rico, for instance, the government has made a concerted effort to build factories in rural areas, which offer jobs for skilled and unskilled workers. Colleges, especially technical training schools, have started up near country villages. As a result, many families are moving out of the overcrowded cities and back to the rural areas, where they now can expect to lead reasonably healthy, productive lives.

Within recent years, the number of immigrants into New York City's Puerto Rican slum, the *barrio,* has decreased. In 1976 more Puerto Ricans moved back to the Island than came to New York. A surprisingly large number of returning families have settled in rural areas and have developed small, livable societies, thanks to concerted planning on the part of the government. But will these families stay in the countryside? Only if special care has been taken to include city amenities in the rural planning.

A family, whom we shall call Munez, was gathered at Kennedy Airport in New York with suitcases, bundles and innumerable large packages from Korvettes and other discount stores. They were on their way back, not to the San Juan slum they had left ten years ago, but to a small new town in the interior of the Island where a textile factory had opened. The factory was surrounded by a small, planned community with well built row houses, stores, a small clinic, schools and, as two of the teenagers pointed out with glee, "a disco and a movie house." The young people had held out longest against their parents' determination to leave the New York slum in the East Bronx where they lived, which was becoming increasingly dilapidated and dangerous. Even though they knew that there would be more and better jobs in the community to which their parents wanted to move, they remembered the old days in the country, where there was nothing to do at the end of the day but look at a flickering TV set, and that was in the local bar where children were usually not admitted. Even with the many hardships of New York, they had become accustomed to city life; to the dances at the community house; the movies that played old horror flicks for one dollar admission after midnight; occasional street fairs with food and rock bands, and all the other fun and games that, along with the leaking ceilings, rats, cockroaches, flooding toilets and constant danger of fire had been part of their existence in the city. Only the older members of the family were really enthusiastic about going back home. The younger ones were openly dubious. "If it's the same dull, boring place we left with a few new houses, we'll come back to New York," one of them said. "Our parents may be happy looking at the same road, the same palm trees and the same faces all the time, but I'm not," one young man said. "If you've seen one coconut, you've seen them all," his sister added. "Sure, things are tough on One-hundred twenty-eighth Street, but I've been learning English. My teacher says I'm pretty bright. I may be able to get into City College here in New York . . . what really is there for me in a small village in the country . . . any country?"

A very popular 1978 movie, *Saturday Night Fever*, dealing with a poor Italian family living in Brooklyn, makes much the same point. Members of that family, including a chronically unemployed father, a bitter, harassed mother, an elderly grandmother and two children, live in an over-crowded flat too small for privacy, too noisy for intimacy

Street Trades

Above: Businessmen and women who cannot afford to rent
stores often sell their goods and services in the streets. This
man shines shoes in the streets of Istanbul. He inherited his
beautiful shoeshine stand from his grandfather. The beauty
of the stand is his advertisement. It works as well as a neon
sign and looks a lot better, too.

Right: Fresh fish for sale on a street in Athens . . .

. . . and above, fresh vegetables on a street in New Delhi, India.

Above right : A shoemaker in Jerusalem doesn't believe the low prices he is offered for his merchandise. Haggling over prices is both a custom and a favorite pastime in many parts of the world.

Below right: These shoppers in Cairo, Egypt, have probably rarely seen the inside of a store. They buy almost everything they need from street merchants, who can afford to charge lower prices because they pay no rent.

There's no point in bargaining with a New York City pretzel and chestnut seller. He'll just mutter something about "stupid tourist" and turn his back.

and constantly in need of repair. There are constant fights between the parents, between the mother and her elderly mother-in-law, and between the parents and the children. But for the nineteen-year-old son, there is an escape from the tension, the frustrations and the constant put-downs by family and employer: the local disco where there are bright lights, loud music and where the young man, as a truly exceptional dancer, gains recognition and praise he gets nowhere else.

There are also the pizza parlors, the bars where a beer still costs twenty-five cents, the social life around the street corners. So most of the young people stay, even though they may be unemployed or the jobs they manage to get and hold are dull and low paid. There is never any suggestion that a move out of New York might provide answers to their problems.

The main character, Tony, whose friend dies in a suicidal fall from a bridge, finally gathers the courage to try to move out of the community in which he was born. He crosses the bridge to find a place to live and work, not in a smaller town where he might be able to find a place for himself, but in Manhattan, where the discos are bigger, the lights brighter and the opportunities just as limited. Still, Manhattan to him is like a foreign country. He doesn't really know if he can survive there . . . and considering the rather bleak picture the moviemaker has painted of urban life, the chances are that he will soon be back at the same old stand in Brooklyn with one more disillusioning experience added to his already difficult young life. But he sees Manhattan as a new Jerusalem—as a place of hope.

Artists, from Charles Dickens to the most recent bestselling author or film maker, from Charlie Chaplin to Robert Altman, may represent cities as cold and hope-destroying cesspools, especially for the poor; but somehow cities are still the magnets that draw individuals and families into their orbit . . . and there they usually remain, even after it becomes evident that city streets are no more paved with gold than country roads.

Even the most desperately poor who live on the streets of Asian cities remain there in spite of government offers to help them return to their rural communities, and often to provide them with a new start should they decide to take up farming again. Recently the Cambodian government forcibly evacuated its large cities and sent former inhabitants to the rural countryside. Those who tried to return were executed. But according to the few eye-witnesses who have managed to escape this most repressive of all modern governments, people still hope that they will somehow, someway, be allowed to return to their city homes.

Mahatma Gandhi's ideas and ideals are revered not only in his native India, but throughout the world. Yet one of his main aspirations—that poverty-stricken Indian families would be able to leave the crowded, inhospitable, filthy city streets and return to communal farming and the arts and crafts their ancestors practiced in the countryside—has never taken root. After the British left their former colony to the Indian government, more families migrated to the cities, rather than less.

Yet it is not only the poor who suffer from the overcrowding of the cities—in India, in the United States or anywhere in the world. For the middle classes and even the rich are reached by the problems that the crowding of cities creates. As urban slums enlarge, they spill over into the areas where the working poor and the middle classes live. These people than flee neighborhoods that they have often lived in for years and where they may have deep roots, to go to the suburbs or to other parts of the city where they do not have such rich associations. And something of the neighborhood quality that people of every age and income level value is lost. Furthermore, the homes and apartments they have left behind soon become a part of urban decay for the same reasons that other slums decay. Then, too, the neighborhoods to which they move may become more crowded—more apartment buildings may be built to house them in place of the one and two family homes that may once have filled the area. And the people who lived there before will be upset because their neighborhood is changing—is no longer the place they knew.

Change is inevitable in the city. And most people know it. But too often it seems to be change for the worse rather than change for the better, and most often it is crowding that makes these changes.

Another area in which crowding is evident for people of all income levels is transportation. The rich banker in his chauffeur-driven limousine is held up just as long in a traffic jam as his secretary is on a bus. And the more people there are in a city, the more cars there are likely to be in the streets to make traffic jams—unless people use bicycles as they do in Amsterdam and Rotterdam, where they have bicycle jams. And if people use public transportation, the more people there are to use that transportation—especially at rush hours—the more crowded those buses, subways and commuter trains are likely to be.

In many American cities with the gas shortage and the high cost of gasoline, more people seem to be using public transportation, and partly at least because there are more people on public conveyances, the transportation itself seems to be getting less dependable and more rundown. Most public transportation in cities is owned and operated by the city, and city finances affect how much can be done to improve it. In cities where budgetary problems are great, buses get old but are not replaced, subway cars decay but remain in service, even when the doors do not all open or the lights all work. And when, at rush hour, these cars are so full of people no one could possibly fall down because there isn't room, the press of bodies is so great, the crowding only makes the decaying cars seem worse.

Few cities can afford whole new transportation systems to help take care of new demands and the increased numbers of people who live in the city or who want to get to the city to work. But Washington, D.C., which does not depend on taxation for everything, as other cities must, because it is partly supported by the national government, is building an extensive new subway system. San Francisco, some years ago, entered into a unique arrangement with its suburbs and together they created BART, a part subway, part above ground rail transportation system. BART has had its problems, but it does get people into the city and around the city with reasonable comfort and expense. New and better transportation can be created for our crowded cities, but it takes a degree of money and urban planning a lot of cities seem unable to bring together.

So it is at all levels that people feel overcrowding—in housing, in stores when they go shopping, in public and private transportation, in just walking down the streets. For some, the presence of great crowds can be exciting—and certainly they make possible the multiple cultural offerings the city presents—but for others the benefits do not always outweigh the disadvantages. Yet people come to the cities: the young to seek better futures, the rich to get richer, the middle class for better jobs, and the poor for reasons that are harder to define.

What is it then that the poor find in the cities? Why do they crowd into already overpopulated areas, leaving rural wastelands behind? What cities have had in the past and still seem to provide is a hope for a better future, no matter how bleak the present may look. People who have seen and heard of the unchanging days and years in their rural communities, who have listened to parents and grandparents tell stories of the past that sound too much like what they see in the present want to be able to tell different stories to their own children and grandchildren. They hope there will be a chance, even if it is a remote one, to change their lives in a place where there's a different view down every street, where someone they know or have heard of has escaped the culture of poverty, and where it may be possible with effort and luck to have a future that's better than the past or the present. So they put up with overcrowding, contribute to it, and only when their best hopes are fulfilled, can the problem of overcrowding be overcome.

11

Police Power

They'll carry guns over my dead body.

> Sir David McNee, Commissioner of
> Scotland Yard, quoted by Associated
> Press, Sept. 7, 1978

The moment we start carrying guns, the people on the other side of the law will use them as well.

> A spokesman for the British Police
> Federation, the union that represents
> all of the country's 114,000 peace
> officers, as quoted by the Associated
> Press, Sept. 7, 1978

There is no such thing as the State
And no one exists alone.
Hunger allows no choice
to the citizen or the police;
We must love one another or die.

> W. H. Auden, in the poem "September, 1939"

When unemployment goes up, our crime rate goes up. When food prices go up, our crime rate goes up. When landlords let unprofitable housing deteriorate, our crime rate goes up. Since unemployment, food prices and the number of abandoned housing units go up constantly, so does our crime rate . . .

> A white New York City police captain
> working out of a high crime ghetto
> precinct

"I watch the kids play cops and robbers," the police captain says sadly. "The robbers always win. Maybe these kids are trying to tell us something."

Apparently they were. Although overall crime statistics in New York City remained fairly steady in 1978, and for a few crimes such as murder, the numbers dropped a little, the crime statistics in his precinct were rising all the time. Unemployment, at less than 7 percent on the national level, was almost 40 percent for young black men under thirty in that district. Food prices at small grocery stores in the neighborhood were at least 20 percent higher than at supermarkets in the prosperous areas of the city. In the captain's precinct, the large stores had closed a long time ago. There had been too many robberies. The small stores, in spite of their higher prices, were barely surviving. Every week another tenement was abandoned by a landlord who insisted that he was losing too much money on his real estate. Most apartments had building code violations, such as insufficient fire protection, too many rats, malfunctioning heating, leaks in ceilings, etc.

The police officers in the precinct were working harder than ever, but they had to concentrate their efforts on major crimes such as murder and arson. What one officer called "small-time burglaries and minor muggings" got very little attention. "We just don't have the time; we have to concentrate on the really violent and dangerous perpetrators in this precinct," the captain said. ("Perpetrator" is a New York City police word that describes the unknown men and women who commit crimes but are not yet caught or identified.)

Many of us believe a myth. We are firmly convinced that the quality of city life is determined by the quality and quantity of police services in the city. Actually, it's the other way around. The quality (if not the quantity) of police services is more often than not determined by the quality of life in that city. Poverty-stricken slum areas, no matter how many police officers are walking the beat, have the highest crime rates. No wonder that some of the police officers get discouraged and often are less and less eager to give their best to a frustrating job.

This is not true for just American cities. It applies to cities in other parts of the world as well. Let's look at two Italian cities: Naples and Bologna. Both have Communist mayors and a predominantly Communist city council. Naples has almost twice as many policemen, for the number of citizens, as Bologna. Yet the crime rate (and the rate of police corruption) in Naples is staggering. Bologna traditionally has had a fairly low rate of violent crime, regardless of the political party in power. In Naples, which is a center for illegal drug traffic, heroin is available on almost every street corner and always has been, regardless of the political party in power. Finding illicit drugs in Bologna would require a week-long search.

What's the difference between these two Italian cities? Naples is a very poor city. It has never recovered from World War II bombings. Families still live in bombed-out buildings and caves on the outskirts of the city. There is almost no adequate low-cost housing. The unemployment rate is staggering, and economic opportunities for young people are almost nonexistent. The education level is low. On the other hand, Bologna, in the north of Italy, is a prosperous university town with heavy industry on the outskirts, offering relatively good, stable jobs to the inhabitants. And most of them have some education.

While hardly anyone in Naples pays taxes (the city fathers have long since given up trying to collect from some of their hard-core debtors), the tax rolls in Bologna are in excellent shape. And for their money, Bologna's law-abiding citizens get some of the best city-sponsored services in the world. There are free medical clinics and free, well-run preschool day care centers in every neighborhood. The parks are so clean that even one abandoned newspaper is noticeable. One can be sure the litter won't be there long. A man with a litter spear will pick it up in minutes and cart it away.

In Naples, there is so much litter and garbage in some

streets and parks that it is difficult to see the sidewalks or the grass. So in Naples the one flourishing industry is crime . . . aided and abetted by police corruption. In Bologna, on the other hand, the quality of life is high and the crime rate correspondingly low, even though the number of policemen patrolling the streets is relatively small. There have been no rumors, even, of police corruption in recent years.

What's more, the quality of police services can deteriorate as the quality of life in a city deteriorates. Let's look at London, England, and Glasgow, Scotland. The London bobby has always been regarded as a model of the gentle, polite and helpful public servant, respected by aristocrat and Cockney laborer alike. London, in spite of some slum areas, has always been a city that valued the quality of urban life. Glasgow, on the other hand, has been looked upon generally by British citizens as an unattractive, polluted, poverty-stricken town. It has high rates of all those evils that seem to be concentrated in neglected urban areas: alcoholism, wife and child battering, drug abuse, gang wars . . . and violent street crime. The average young citizen of Glasgow has disliked and distrusted the police for as long as anyone can remember. Insults and catcalls hurled at policemen were common even a hundred years ago.

In London, until quite recently, it was inconceivable that a citizen would call a bobby a "pig." Policemen were expected to deal with difficult situations using diplomatic skills rather than physical violence. And most bobbies lived up to expectations.

To this day, policemen, in Glasgow as well as in London, do not carry guns. The only weapon they have is a nightstick, and they are expected to use that as sparingly as possible. Any incident involving what seems to be "excessive" police violence is investigated carefully. If a policeman loses his temper and deals in blows instead of conciliatory words, he is reprimanded, and if the incident is repeated, demoted or fired. But in Glasgow, there have always been many more complaints about police attacks than there have been in London, and some of these complaints have been investigated only superficially, or not at all.

The state of peace between London bobbies and London citizens has produced some statistics that would delight any mayor's heart. The violent death rate among London bobbies was among the lowest in the world. If a breath of scandal touched the police department, the public was not just outraged, it was astounded. The usual reaction was: "There must have been some mistake." What's more, the violent death rate among "perpetrators" was also very low. Burglars didn't carry guns either. They might put up a fight to keep from being arrested . . . but they usually used only their fists. Criminals knew that they could expect absolutely no mercy from the courts if they were caught carrying any kind of weapon. It was simply safer to commit crimes unarmed.

In recent years all that has changed. The change began when dark-skinned immigrants started to arrive in London in ever growing numbers. They were usually citizens from Great Britain's former colonies and could, therefore, live anywhere the British flag flew, London included.

The London police had been carefully trained in civility; but until recently this civility needed to be extended only to those who looked, thought and talked like them. Bobbies had received little preparation for dealing with the racial and ethnic tensions that begin developing in the center of their city. When England was still an almost all white, homogeneous country, it was fashionable to talk about racism—in the United States or South Africa, but hardly ever at home.

London, like most cities had, of course, always contained ghettos of poverty. But the poor, like the rich, were expected to behave in a way that can only be described as "British." They could complain, organize political parties, occasionally march on Parliament (never on Buckingham Palace where the royal family lived), but protests were to remain nonviolent, and if possible, reasonably polite. The new black and brown minorities were not "British" however. When they protested job discrimination, intolerable housing conditions and lack of equal educational opportunities, they were not always polite. They screamed out four letter words that, in England, were rarely heard in private, never mind at a street corner rally. They insulted the Queen, they threw garbage, and generally behaved in a way that was quite unacceptable to the white British citizens (especially middle-aged white British workers) in general, and the police in particular.

The police had a weapon against this kind of behavior, which they considered unacceptable: a law that allows a policeman to arrest a person who is "loitering with the *intention* of committing a crime." That's the kind of law that the framers of the American Constitution would not allow on the books. In the United States one can be arrested only for what one *does,* not for what someone else thinks one might intend to do. Even laws that were aimed at preventing people from conspiring to do something illegal have usually been found to be unconstitutional in the United States. But, in England, an even older democracy than the United States, people had sufficient faith in their public servants to allow them to judge whether someone was loitering at a street corner to whistle at pretty girls or whether he was planning to rob a grocery store. Until the new immigrants started to arrive in large numbers, the bobbies justified that faith. Arrests under the "loitering with intention" law were rare indeed. But the number of such arrests (and convictions) rose drastically right along with immigration. And those arrested turned out to be almost exclusively young black or brown males. They could not afford good lawyers, so some pleaded guilty in return for a less severe verdict from the courts. Those who decided to defend themselves found that judges tended to believe the policemen. After all, British policemen were known to be honest, fair and not overeager to throw citizens into jail, weren't they?

The arrests infuriated the black communities in London. They, like their American brothers in many cities, began to look on the bobby as an enemy. The policeman found that, instead of being called "sir," he was now being addressed as "pig." Bands of youngsters oinked at him as he walked his beat. Some of the young suspects began to resist arrest. Police began to use greater force. Soon charges of police brutality were being voiced by the black and brown communities and by their friends in the white establishment. The feeling of distrust became just plain hatred between young immigrants and policemen, and this soon spread to some young whites. Right now, in London, there are many policemen who want to carry guns on their rounds. Ten years ago, most British policemen disliked and feared guns almost as much as the rest of the British population. England, after all, has one of the strictest gun laws in the world.

Not only new immigrants, but various terrorist groups have now begun to operate in London as well as many other European cities. In many ways, the London bobbies are less well prepared to face the threat of the bomber, arsonist and murderer than the police in other countries, who are more accustomed to seemingly irrational violence.

In August of 1978, a Palestine Liberation Front terrorist group attacked a bus that was carrying the crew of an Israeli airliner to Heathrow Airport. One stewardess was killed, another seriously wounded. The Israeli government complained bitterly to the British government that the English no-gun policy had allowed the incident to happen. "What's a policeman without a gun to do when he has to confront a terrorist who is armed to the teeth?" one Israeli asked an American reporter in London. "Not only will they not allow their own police to carry guns, they even take weapons away from our security men when they enter the country. Are we supposed to just stand by and allow that to happen?"

As a result of this attack, British authorities issued guns to police officers assigned to airport details. Not only were guns issued, but some of the police officers also began to carry heavy duty rifles. For several days, buses carrying Israeli plane crews to the London airport were followed by a British *tank,* fully manned, with machine guns clearly visible. But the British stood firm on not allowing civilians (foreign security forces, as well as their own citizens) to carry guns.

Today there are many British citizens who would like to be able to carry guns for self-protection against black or brown immigrants, foreign terrorists, local hoodlums or anyone else who represents a threat to "law and order," a term that has become fashionable in England when it has almost ceased to be an overriding issue in the United States.

There's no question that the quality of life has deteriorated in London. Tourists are being warned not to walk alone in the parks at night. Certain sections of the city are off-limits to any kind of nighttime walking. The rate of street crime does not begin to approach that of any major American city, but some oldtime Londoners are now echoing the words of their American cousins: "I am afraid to go out after dark."

A drop in confidence in the police, accompanied by lowered police morale, has become evident. In August of 1978 for the first time in years, charges of corruption were levied against several high officers in the London police force. A committee was investigating these charges and apparently finding them to be at least partially true. (At the time this book was being written).

Unemployment, high food prices and slum conditions were increasing in London, as well as in Naples, Detroit and some sections of New York City. And so were crimes. And so were complaints about the police.

There is at least one country in the world where the police seem to manage with a minimum of problems. That country is Japan, which also has the lowest crime rate of any urbanized country. In Tokyo, unescorted women can walk at night without fear. People still leave their doors unlocked when they leave for a weekend. Bicycles and motorcycles are parked in front of stores and office buildings without locks. The main gripe riders of the crowded Tokyo subway have is that a woman occasionally is pinched by a male who disappears into the mob at the subway exit before she can confront him and give him a piece of her mind.

Tokyo police work in twenty hour "turns," meaning that they are on duty for twenty hours at a stretch during a four-day week, and then are off two days. Much of that twenty hours is spent on street patrols. Policemen, in twos, walk city blocks, checking very politely anyone who looks even faintly suspicious. They get to know the people who live and work on their beats. Many of these officers spend most of their professional lives walking the same four or five blocks so that they come to know more about what goes on there than most of the residents. The Japanese word for "patrolman" is *"omawari-san"* or, literally, "Mr. Walk-about." Having the same patrolman walking the same street month after month, year after year, seems to be one of the reasons for Japan's incredibly low crime rate.

There are other reasons, of course. *The Wall Street Journal* of August 9, 1979 cites the near total ban on firearms owned by civilians. The item quotes a thirty-two-year-old veteran of the police force, Isao Yokoo, as stating that he "has never drawn his pistol while on duty except for target practice, although he recalls that once a fellow officer fired a shot as he chased a kidnapper during the American occupation of Japan."

Also, there is little use of illegal drugs, mostly because of the stigma that Japanese society attaches to those drugs, but partly because the criminal justice system deals very harshly with pushers.

But the most important reason of all is perhaps the fact that in Japan the criminal is never glamorized. If a Japanese commits a crime and is caught, he and his family face social ostracism and public humiliation, a loss of face, which most Japanese fear more than punishment. "One indication of this cultural trait is that when wrongdoers make a sincere statement of contrition for their misdeeds, authorities are much more lenient with whatever penalties they mete out," the *Wall Street Journal* states.

Traditionally, Japanese have had a great respect for authority. This attitude in itself may create problems politically. It made possible a very restrictive government for many years before World War II. But there are also benefits, and these benefits become especially evident in Japanese crime prevention programs. Citizens cooperate with law enforcement agencies to a degree that would astonish most Americans.

For instance, the walk-about policemen visit every resident and business in their area twice a year, and collect the kinds of data that would make most American citizens feel their privacy was being severely invaded. Even in between visits from the police, Japanese routinely report any suspicious activity in their neighborhood and many join prevention associations whose members volunteer to help safety campaigns and other programs. Some of these associations have lately sprung up in some American cities, and they seem to be quite effective there as well.

But most important of all, the Japanese seem to consider the law as a form of natural and needed order, and give the safety of the whole community the same importance they do personal safety and prosperity. As a result of this attitude, they do indeed seem to be both safe and prosperous.

12

The Battle Zones

In some of America's largest cities there are areas that should be declared war zones . . . they have become a no man's land of violence and terror . . . they even look the part, like battle fields, with their abandoned buildings, shattered windows, doors stripped off the hinges and scattered litter.

The one-time melting pots of America have become cauldrons of frustration that one day will boil over if the rest of the nation remains indifferent.

Any city, however small, is, in fact, divided into two: one city for the rich and the other for the poor. They are at war with each other.

Columnists Jack Anderson and Les Witten, September 1977

The United States is the clear leader among modern, stable democratic nations in its rates of homicide, assault, rape and robbery. . . .

We have endured and survived other cycles of violence in our history. Today, however, we are more vulnerable to violence than ever before. Two-thirds of our people live in urban areas, where violence especially thrives . . . Men are no longer capable of solitary living and individual self-defense: men must live together and depend on one another to observe the laws and keep the peace. . . .

THE FINAL REPORT OF THE NATIONAL COMMISSION ON THE CAUSES AND PREVENTION OF VIOLENCE, Praeger Publishers, 1970

Here they sing of gunmen in the pubs. . . .

> Betty Williams of Belfast, Northern
> Ireland, co-founder with Mairead
> Corrigan of the Peace People and
> winner with Miss Corrigan of the
> 1976 Nobel Peace Prize

Poverty is often off the beaten track. For many of us the urban poor exist only as statistics. It's very hard to translate vast numbers of people (about 50 million in this country alone) into separate human beings: a hungry, neglected child, a young man who has never been able to find a job and has given up trying to find one, a woman hopelessly chasing cockroaches and rats in a cramped tenement flat that is unbearably hot in the summer and freezing in the winter. These people tend to live in the rotting centers of large cities, where few of us have any reason to visit. We may pass them fleetingly in a train or car, going from somewhere to somewhere else. Some of us now instinctively lock our car doors when we know we will be forced to stop at red lights as we pass through those garbage-littered streets, where groups of young men gather at street corners, looking bored, sullen and, somehow, menacing. The sight of these streets makes us uncomfortable: we may feel a little guilty and more than a little afraid. We have reasons for both feelings, because the invisible poor are forcing themselves more and more on our attention and the method they use is often random, apparently unreasoning violence. This war of the cities is occurring not just in America, but in many Western Europe countries as well.

For instance, on a hot night in July of 1977, all the lights went out in New York City. The government and the electric company will probably disagree about the basic causes for the blackout for years to come, but the results were evident immediately. An orgy of looting, burning and general mayhem destroyed parts of the city . . . while policemen and firemen stood by helplessly. Policemen attempting to stop looters were attacked by gangs of young people. Merchandise retrieved from one band of looters was quickly scooped up by another. Firemen attempting to put out fires set by arsonists in stores, and even in apartments, were stoned by mobs and had to retreat to watch flames consume whole blocks at a time.

The violence was so much more frightening because it was so unexpected. Several years earlier, a power blackout had occurred that put out the lights of cities all along the Northeast Coast of the United States. Not only had there been very little looting, the residents of large Eastern cities, from New York to Boston, astounded the world by their cheerful cooperation, their helpfulness to neighbors and strangers, and their patience in coping with their many difficulties. A check by reporters disclosed that, astonishingly, there had been fewer injuries due to muggings, rape and general mayhem in the affected cities during the blackout than during a normal night. There were also fewer arrests, not because police officers were unable to do their jobs, but because, apparently, very few individuals were taking advantage of the situation to loot or steal. In a few years all of that had changed. As one welfare mother put it to a reporter: "Pretty soon the lights won't have to go out for trouble to start." This is true for many Western European cities as well as those in the United States. Why? Have people suddenly changed? The chances are that in one way, at least, they have.

During the decades of the '50s and '60s, here and in Europe, government officials seemed to be sending a message of hope to city dwellers. "We know things are bad for you," they seemed to be saying. "But just wait a while . . . we are doing everything we can to make things better."

Urban renewal, everywhere, was expected to provide decent housing for those who were living in the worst slums. There would be more jobs, better education, more accessible health care for the poor. In the United States we declared a war on poverty. It was a war we expected to win. We didn't. Here, as in many other countries, most of the promises were just not fulfilled. Slums were indeed torn down, but somehow much of the new housing never got off the drawing boards, and the developments that were built were often so badly planned that they became instant slums.

In almost all urban areas throughout the world, unemployment has indeed dropped during the past decade . . . but not among the young and the unskilled, whose hopes had been raised by all the earlier promises. Psychologists have long known that broken promises lead to frustration, and frustration can lead to violence. What's true for individuals is also true for groups. It may well be that during that earlier blackout in New York, the inner city slum dwellers still expected their lives to get better. By the time July 1977 rolled around, they no longer believed that.

It's a long way from Harlem and the South Bronx in New York to Belfast, Northern Ireland. The cityscape in Belfast is similar to that described by columnists Anderson and Whitten: half burned-out, uninhabited buildings, empty, littered lots in which starving cats and dogs compete for food with rats, an occasional building still standing and occupied by families who desperately want to leave but have nowhere to go. The strife is ostensibly religious, but is actually based in poverty and a sense of powerlessness. And in Belfast there is an additional monument to violence: across a once-busy thoroughfare, two twelve-foot walls made up of abandoned and bricked-in buildings, rubble and cement, and topped by two more feet of rusty barbed wire, face each other across a no-man's-land. The street is empty except for an occasional British tank or a jeep filled with soldiers, their machine guns in plain sight.

Belfast's population is deeply weary of the violence, as are most of the people who live in America's inner cities. But the violence continues, with terrorist gangs in Ireland and street gangs in New York finding new recruits every year, as young people who have lost hope for a reasonably happy and productive future join to take out their frustrations on the rest of the people and each other.

Is this the war of the poor against the rich that Anderson and Whitten saw in the future? Not really, most experts say. One of the saddest aspects of urban violence is that frequently the poor turn against the poor: neighbor steals from neighbor, muggers prey on the elderly in their own block. A study done in Philadelphia points out that most rapists attack women of their own race living in their own neighborhoods. Other studies done in Italy, France and England seem to confirm this impression.

Actually, the report of the National Commission on the Causes and Prevention of Violence, commissioned after the assassinations of President John F. Kennedy, Robert Kennedy and Martin Luther King, was one of two ordered by the U.S. government in response to our increasing fears that the forces of urban terror were growing too strong to handle. The first, completed in 1968, was called the *Report of the National Advisory Commission on Civil Disorders.* It concerned itself more with the social rather than individual, psychological causes of violence. Its principal prediction was that the United States was separating into two societies: the white and the black.

In 1978, ten years later, the *New York Times* in a week-long series, took an exhaustive look at this conclusion and found it to be inaccurate. The division was not between the races, but between the rich and the poor, the newspaper's editors concluded, echoing Anderson and Whitten. In fact, black communities had split. As the *Times* put it: "One of the most striking developments in American society in the past decade has been the abandonment of the ghetto by millions of upwardly mobile blacks. In some cases, they now live side by side with white families in similar economic circumstances. More often they have moved to middle-class black neighborhoods, which have expanded in almost every American city. The houses and yards are indistinguishable from white communities. And, in many instances, so are the attitudes of the residents." (*New York Times,* Feb. 28, 1978.)

There are some social critics, both white and black,

who blame the new black middle-class for "ignoring the plight of their poverty-stricken brothers and sisters." But others point out, with more justice, that all of us have ignored the invisible poor, regardless of race. They ask why a black lawyer or professor or businessman should be more concerned with the black welfare mother and the black unemployed teenager than the white lawyer or professor or businessman. Why do we expect more from our black fellow citizens than we expect from our white ones?

Yet, though the split between rich and poor exists, the battle seems not to be between the two, but contained within the poor neighborhood. When the July blackout occurred in New York, the gangs of looters and arsonists hardly ever left the few square blocks in which they lived. They wrecked and stole from their neighborhood stores. They burned down the building next door. In a way, they seemed to be turning on themselves more than on those others: the people in the suburbs who had never met the invisible poor of the inner cities.

The same pattern is true of many riots that have been occurring in urban areas in Western Europe. Often it's the homes in which the rioters themselves live that are destroyed. Nowhere is this more evident than in Belfast, where the more affluent parts of the city remain relatively untouched while the strictly segregated Catholic and Protestant slums have been burned and bombed.

Obviously it's not easy to find someone who will answer the question: "Why do you want to destroy your own neighborhood? Does that not make your problem worse, rather than better?" But in Belfast several young members of the Provisional IRA (the only terrorist organization in the world that seems to have a public relations department that a reporter can call to arrange for interviews) were more than willing to speak. "I have no chance for a job or for a halfway decent place to live," one teenager said. "My parents think that it's the will of God for us to have to live the way we do. Well, I don't. And every time I throw a gasoline bomb, I'm telling someone that I just am not going to take it anymore. I'm not going to live that way . . . I'd rather be dead."

In New York a young woman said that she had participated in the looting spree during the blackout. She was upset afterward that another store in which she had a part-time job had burned to the ground and that the drug store where she got her mother's prescription medicine had been emptied and smashed. "Where am I going to work and what's Mom going to do for medicine?" she asked. But she added that the next time there was a blackout she's going on a looting spree again. "I felt better that night than I have in years," she said. She didn't even want many of the items she took from the stores and had no intention of selling them. "It just felt great to be able to go into a store and take anything I wanted out with me," she added. "Almost like the kind of Christmas I used to expect when I still believed in Santa Claus."

The violence in our cities is terrifying to most of us. Many who never have contact with the invisible poor have reacted by demanding stiffer jail sentences, the return to the death penalty, and detention in jail of those who have committed violent crimes. Still others have bought guns. Gun sales rose to unprecedented heights in the United States in 1976 and 1977 . . . and so did the rate of crimes committed with guns (including family fights that ended in death and injury) and accidents involving guns. But it is clear that the wider dissemination of weapons among members of the middle class has not stopped violence. Indeed, in countries where there are strict gun control laws (Japan, England, Sweden, New Zealand and Turkey) urban violence and individual violent crimes are considerably less frequent than in the United States. As the National Commission on the Causes and Prevention of Violence stated, America leads the civilized world in crimes directed against people. And one of the recommendations made by this Commission was the enactment and enforcement of much stricter gun laws. But like almost all other recommendations made by this distinguished group of professionals and laymen—headed by Milton Eisenhower, brother of the late President Eisenhower—the recommendation has been ignored. Indeed President Lyndon Johnson, who saw a preliminary report made by the Commission, tried to cut off the group's funds because he knew that the suggested solutions would be expensive and unpopular.

And President Nixon, when presented with the final version of the report, made it public only after saying that most of the recommendations went entirely against his own convictions.

Yet the very people who do not want to listen to unpopular suggestions about gun control or about curbing violence in other ways, because it might cost money, do have to worry about violence themselves. Though most of the crimes committed by the poor take place in poor communities, there are those who make war on the elderly and on the middle class and wealthy of all areas. And these are not only the poor. There are rich children who steal and mug for kicks, perhaps for some of the same reasons the poor do—because they are neglected by parents who are too busy. People in all city neighborhoods are experiencing increases of all kinds of crimes, from petty shoplifting to rape and murder, some by people of their own area, and some by people from other neighborhoods. Crime in the streets may not be the issue now that it once was, but a life lived in fear anywhere is not a life lived to its fullest measure.

Recently New York City experienced an epidemic of bank robberies. These occurred in every neighborhood in the city. In some cases the holdup persons were armed, in other cases they may have only pretended to be armed. But because no one knew for sure if the arms were real or not, the robberies were for the most part successful. And whether people realize it or not, everyone suffers when any business is robbed. The cost for the services of that organization must go up to cover the losses incurred.

Yet people still don't want to hear or know about what might be causing urban violence regardless of where it occurs. A truly sensational murder will make headlines, but the daily mayhem in many of our urban areas appears in the paper as a one paragraph item, if at all. The same is true, incidentally, in most Western European cities where urban crimes are now rising at an alarming rate.

In London districts where East Indians, many of whom fled from political terror and violence in Uganda, are crowded into wretched slum flats, there are stabbings nightly and beatings that are rarely reported. Again, this kind of violence has become so much a part of the British urban scene that it has come to be considered an almost normal part of city life.

French Algerians, settled in the poorest and most crowded parts of Paris and Marseilles, have met a similar fate. So have Moluccans, who have settled in one part of Amsterdam. Even though these immigrants are citizens of the countries in which they live, they are considered outsiders. What they do to each other is of very little interest to the insiders. Only when they break out of their ghetto, when they commit crimes against the rest of the citizens, do they begin to make headlines. South Moluccans in Amsterdam have been a source of trouble to each other and the Dutch police ever since they left their home area of Indonesia. When Holland gave up that territory and the country became independent, the new government forcibly expelled much of the Moluccan minority. These people went to the Netherlands and were ignored. However, when a small group of these men kidnapped a train full of Dutch citizens and a school full of children, they suddenly made worldwide headlines. Most of us, until that day, had not even known who or what a Moluccan was.

Our ignorance about our own poor, of course, is understandable. The poor are indeed invisible and isolated, and few of us have any reason to seek them out. We all have problems in our own lives, and the problems of a group of people who don't seem to touch us seem irrelevant in our day-to-day existence. What's more, there is apparently very little that any of us, as individuals, can do to change what's happening to those untold millions in cities throughout the world who don't know where their next meal, or their next night's shelter, will come from.

But when we look at the violence in the cities throughout the world, when we are forced to walk the streets of New York, Detroit, Montgomery, Dallas, San Francisco, Paris, London, Munich or Belfast at night, it's important to remember that there are root causes that motivate the people we fear so much, and that these causes are not just in their own heads, but also in the circumstances under which they live.

Not very many people read that Violence Commission report; so it might be worthwhile to sum up its conclusions, which apply not just to the United States, but to many countries throughout the world:

1) Violent crimes are chiefly the problem of the cities; and there violent crimes are committed mainly by the young, poor, male inhabitants of the ghetto slums.

2) In the slums, increasingly powerful social forces are generating rising levels of violent crime that, unless checked, threaten to turn our cities into defensive, fearful societies.

3) An improved criminal justice system is required to contain the growth of violent crime, but only progress towards urban reconstruction can reduce the strength of the crime-causing forces in the inner city and thus reverse the direction of our present crime trends.

All of this seems like a very large order, but there are some individual attitudes we can reconsider and perhaps change. Poet W. H. Auden may have been putting the case too strongly when he told us that we must "love each other or die." Love actually may be too much . . . and also too little. We must learn to care about each other . . . not for noble, unselfish reasons alone, but for our own sense of security and safety. Furthermore as long as we sing of gunmen in the pubs, as long as we make a hero of the gunfighter, be he Dirty Harry, Shaft, or the Irish Republican Army man in a Belfast pub, violence will be part of our daily lives—and it won't get better over the years, it will get worse.

13

The Wild Children

I've got a hooligan class of fourteen year olds. I was trying like a conscientious fool to get them talking about their own interests. Before I know where I am, this pathetic, pixilated child is halfway through a description of how to boobytrap a car. Some of the others are correcting him on points of detail. It was educationally very high grade . . . plenty of pupil involvement, sponteneity of ideas, combined with orderly discussion, scope for follow-up activities. . . .

I was coming home from school today and I met a child from the backward class, the hopeless ones. He had a mongrel dog that used to follow him backwards and forwards to school. He'd been attacked by a gang of the other crowd. They'd hung the dog on a lamppost and set fire to it. It won't make the newspapers or the press bulletins—it can scarcely compete with the latest hooded corpse or pub massacre. But that child's soul has been butchered, as surely as if they'd taken a meat cleaver to him. This is the day he'll remember when he's putting a bullet into somebody else. There are thousands like him. . . .

> The speaker is Daisy, a Belfast
> school teacher in *Spokesong*, a
> prize-winning play by Stewart Parker

Frightening enough when they are alone or in pairs, youths in gangs are a formidable engine of mayhem. Today's urban gangs commit roughly 25% of juvenile crime, and they are better organized than ever, more heavily armed and less queasy about the blood they spill.

> *Time*, July 11, 1977

Quietly, and with much the same anguish and bewilderment that Americans feel, the Soviet Union is struggling with problems of street crime, teenage gangs, and juvenile delinquency.

Murders, rape, beatings, muggings and burglaries now occur in Moscow and other cities with a frequency that arouses concern among some officials and ordinary citizens.

New York Times, March 5, 1978

Until fairly recently most of us met them only in novels and films, but they were probably there all along: the wild children of the world's urban ghettos. In *Oliver Twist* they were the pathetic, yet somehow courageous and enterprising waifs led into a life of crime by evil adults. In *West Side Story* they were the violent and often vicious gang members who still seemed occasionally honorable and glamorous, since they were defending their turf or their fellows with those knives and guns they carried at all times. They were ignored by their parents, mistreated by the police and misunderstood by gullible social workers. Even in a film like *The Blackboard Jungle,* the violent kids were only the bad apples in an otherwise normal urban high school. Today they are in the headlines all over the world. They are still often mistreated and misunderstood, but they are certainly not considered either pathetic, courageous or glamorous. And no one can ignore them.

Fourteen-year-olds in Belfast do considerably worse than burning dogs hung on lamp posts. Some have been involved in brutal killings. A gang of schoolboys viciously beat the then thirteen-year-old son of Nobel Peace Prize winner, Betty Williams. He suffered serious kidney damage, but his mother says: "It could have been worse." Two of his young relatives have been murdered, one by Protestants and the other by Catholics. There are many teenagers in Northern Ireland who are as repelled by violence as their counterparts in Paris, Rome, Detroit or San Francisco, but gang members have a way of forcing them to join up. It's called "kneecapping," a shot with a pistol through the knee-cap that leaves the victim a cripple for life. The threat of that kind of treatment has forced many a fourteen or fifteen year old to join a terrorist street gang against his better instincts and common sense.

Pressures on teenagers in other countries are similar. *Time* quotes a young Puerto Rican on why he found peer pressure to enlist in a gang irresistible: "Protection man, protection. I was a little skinny kid and was tired of having hassles. You don't last long if you don't join a club. If you do, you can always count on having someone stand up for you." Echoes of *West Side Story?* Not really. In New York City, members of a gang sat on either side of a man in a subway, stuck him with knives from both sides, robbed him and kept him propped up until they got off the train. To get at members of rival gangs or other real or imagined enemies, some of these teenagers have invaded hospital emergency rooms. In a Bronx hospital one gang was kept out of an operating room, where an "enemy" was being treated for a gunshot wound, by a knife-wielding young surgeon until the police arrived to haul everyone off to Juvenile Hall. In Los Angeles, there is one gang called "The Cripples" with a female auxiliary called "The Crippets." A member is initiated only after he has furnished proof that he has seri-ously injured someone. The someone often turns out to be old or handicapped, or both.

Nor are American or Northern Irish cities the only ones threatened by the teenage gang members and their even younger brothers and sisters. London used to be one of the safest cities on earth. One could walk through Hyde Park at three o'clock in the morning and meet only an occasional friendly policeman or an enthusiastic supporter of prohibition, socialism, vegetarianism or fundamentalist religion, setting up his soap box for what he hoped would be a spirited debate later in the day. Now no sensible Londoner would walk alone in Hyde Park, or any other British city park for that matter, after dark. Gangs of teenagers, often dressed in outlandish costumes, have been known to rob and beat up tourists and local residents severely enough to send them to the hospital. There are more knifings, muggings and robberies in England now than ever before. Even though England has one of the strongest gun laws in the world, the gangs have weapons. "We learned to smuggle them in from the kids in Belfast," one sixteen year old said. "After all, they've got the same gun laws in Northern Ireland."

In Rome, the favorite ploy of the juvenile criminal is purse snatching—from motorcycles. They work in pairs. As victims are crossing the street, two young men will speed up on either side and lunge for a purse, pocketbook or camera. Before the victim knows what's happened, the robbers are off at full speed. Often they empty out the purse and throw it away before the victim has even had a chance to get off the ground and call the police.

The case of Mrs. Betty Gardner, an eighty-three-year-old American tourist, was not typical only because she died as a result of the attack. Her mistake was hanging onto her purse until she fell and was dragged along the street by one of the two cyclists, who did not slow down. When she finally let go, her hip was broken. She was taken to a hospital and died as a result of her injuries. The Italian papers did not report the story . . . purse snatching has become so common that it is hardly ever mentioned—and besides, a dead tourist is bad for business.

American papers ran the story, however. And Italian police warn tourists to stay away from youth-gang-plagued areas of the city. The problem is that the streets on which the youthful criminals operate are usually the ones that the tourist has come to Italy to see: the once super-elegant Via Veneto with its luxury hotels and excellent sidewalk cafes, the streets at the top and bottom of the Spanish Steps, and the one that runs along the Fountain of Trevi. But with one purse snatching every forty-five minutes around the clock, many visitors to Rome now do their sightseeing in large groups. As the Italian police have pointed out, Japanese visitors, who tend to stick with their tour groups, are rarely robbed, even though they often carry a great deal of expensive and tempting camera equipment.

The basic Italian street gang is not politically moti-vated. "Many foreigners ask me if these gangs are fascist or communist," a Naples policeman said. "They are neither . . . they are battling for control of a street block or a piazza. Many of these gangs extract 'protection' money from the merchants in the area . . . and they don't want compe-tition from another group. It seems that if more than one gang starts to terrorize a business community, they either hire private guards with guns or they call in the police. One gang they'll put up with—as an unpleasant and necessary nuisance—but not two."

A priest in Belfast told a similar story. "Sure the gangs are either Catholic or Protestant," he said. "Everything in this town is divided along religious lines—so why not the juvenile gangs? But they are after protection money—not political goals." The owner of a Jewish bakery ("the best bagels and rye bread in Belfast," she advertised) found that out. She had been visited by representatives of two groups: one Catholic and one Protestant for "contribu-tions" to their respective causes. She had turned both down because, as she put it, "I can't take sides in your religious wars." Her shop was blown up by a bomb, and a note was left telling her that her "protection" had been "withdrawn" because of her uncooperative attitude. To this day, she does not know which of the two gangs wiped out her livelihood. "It could have been either," she said sadly as she looked over the wreckage of her formerly prosperous business and made plans to leave Northern Ireland. "The kids look so much alike. I wonder how they tell each other apart."

South America, too, has its share of wild children, even in those countries that have enjoyed relative prosperity. Since 1969, Brazil has achieved one of the world's most spectacular growth rates. The standard of living has been going up steadily in Rio de Janeiro and Brasilia, the coun-try's modern capital. The middle-class is growing and thriv-

Slum Housing

Above: Somehow people manage to live in some of the most crowded, unsanitary, unpleasant homes . . . anywhere in the world. This large family shares a tin and tar paper hut outside of Calcutta, India. They are better off than some. Many in Calcutta just live in the streets.

Above right: Because of the extreme housing shortage in Egypt, many families live in the City of the Dead, a cemetery that was still used to bury people fifty years ago. Now it houses thousands of families.

Below right: This ancient street in Athens, Greece, may lack modern improvements, but it generally works well as a community. Many of the families who live here today have owned these houses for more than two hundred years.

Above left: Where city space is in short supply, people make their homes wherever they can find a suitable spot. These families in Hong Kong live in boats in the harbor. People also live on boats in Amsterdam, London and a few coastal towns in California.

Above: Living on a boat in Hong Kong may be a lot more pleasant than living in this recently built, over-crowded, filthy slum tenement. Similar government-sponsored housing projects for the poor exist all over the world, including the United States.

Below left: These nineteenth century houses in Istanbul are lovely to look at and have a beautiful view of the city. What they do not have are such amenities as electricity and plumbing. Also, they probably have not been looked at by a fire inspector since they were built.

New York City has its slums too. In many cases landlords now
abandon decrepit buildings and leave tenants without electricity,
water or other services.

ing. There are modern skyscrapers going up in many of Brazil's booming cities. Night clubs and movie theaters are filled to capacity every night. There are expensive American and German automobiles clogging the city streets. But amid the relative luxury, there are more than two million children, ranging in age from infants to teenagers, who have been abandoned by their destitute parents.

Many of these parents have come to the cities from the countryside, hoping for better opportunities, but since they are unskilled and often illiterate, the relative prosperity of the Brazilian middle-class has not rubbed off on them. Many of the women bear a child every year—and they have no way of feeding their families. So, they leave infants on the steps of churches and other public places; they turn toddlers out of doors with just the clothes on their backs; they leave older children at street corners with instructions not to try to find their parents. More than one hundred children are abandoned every month. The youngsters themselves have coined a phrase for this form of abandonment: "joining the struggle." And only the strongest and most ruthless survive the struggle. They form gangs that prey on each other, as well as the more prosperous.

The abandoned children are often sick and some die. Some grow into adulthood stunted and illiterate. In one of the few private orphanges that have been set up to care for some of these children, the average IQ of the youngsters range between fifty and seventy. In the United States, such scores are classified as indicating that the child is mentally retarded. Meanwhile the population of Brazil is expected to increase to one billion in less than a century. And the population explosion is probably going to take place mostly among the very poor.

Brazil, which spends billions on economic development, spent only 38 million in 1978 on children's services, and even this money did not go to the poorest of the poor. Of course, many of the abandoned children have turned to crime as the only way of life.

In America's largest cities, the wild children are now

in control of many of the schools. In Europe this has not yet happened—although many educators fear that it may in the future. The high school seen on ABC's top-rated TV series, *Welcome Back Kotter,* with its mischievious, lovable "sweathogs" is a myth. The truth can be seen at Morris High School in the South Bronx, New York. All entrances have been sealed, even though this represents a fire hazard. There are other, more immediate dangers: mayhem and murder. So there is only one entrance into the building, with a security guard at the door turning back anyone who tries to enter without proper identification. Inside there are five more guards who communicate with each other on walkie-talkies. Classroom doors are locked after classes enter (another fire hazard), and there are no more study halls: too many bloody fights. The lockers have been removed; they were used as a storage area for weapons and drugs. One can hardly believe that high quality education can take place under such conditions.

Some schools have installed a closed circuit TV system, along with guards. Memphis, Tennessee, which is spending a sizable percentage of its educational budget on school security, reported 680 assaults in 1977, 144 of them directed against teachers.

In fact, attacks against teachers are increasing at a faster rate than those against students. A study, released in early 1978 by the National Institute on Education, "Violent Schools . . . Safe Schools" reports that a quarter of all American schools, about 20,500 of them, have serious problems with vandalism, personal attack and thievery. In 1978, the report estimates, one out of every nine secondary school students will have something stolen in a typical month. Even worse, one out of every eighty will be physically attacked during the same period. Among America's secondary school teachers (one million in all), 5,200 will be attacked by students, and one fifth of them seriously injured. Vandalism costs were estimated at more than half a billion for the year.

The youth gang members in *West Side Story* laughed

at their teachers and at other authority figures—they didn't mug them, stab them or shoot them. And, except for increasing security forces inside schools—spending precious dollars for armed guards instead of more psychological counselors, remedial teachers and new books and other educational tools—no one seems to be sure about how to combat the rising tide of school violence. Many parents give the physical danger to their children as the reason for abandoning the cities for the suburbs, and others who stay in the city take their children out of the public schools system and send them to parochial or other private schools. Several bills have been introduced in the U.S. Congress to make at least part of the cost of a private education tax deductible. As more parents protest that they are forced to pay increasingly higher taxes for an educational system they can't use, such laws may indeed pass in the future. Then there would, of course, be even less money for public schools.

What can be done about the wild children, here and in other cities throughout the world? No one seems to have devised a workable solution. In America, state legislatures are considering increasing numbers of bills that would treat violent offenders as adults in the courts. Murder would be murder; assault would be assault, whether committed by a fourteen year old or a thirty year old. But even those who lobby for such laws admit that their effect would be limited to taking the most violent of the young criminals off the streets for longer periods of time. Our adult prison system tends to operate a revolving door: many of those serving prison sentences go right back to street crime when they are released. There is no reason to suppose that a teenager in an adult prison would act any differently from his older brother.

There are some large cities in the world that seem to be remarkably free of street crime. For some—Stockholm, Sweden, Olso, Norway, and Zurich, Switzerland—the reasons are obvious: a relatively small, racially and religiously homogeneous population, with little poverty and no slum ghettos. In others these surface reasons do not apply. Istanbul, Turkey is a melting pot of many ethnic, racial and religious minorities. Poverty is everywhere. There are thousands of temporary huts, called "gichicondas" by the Turks. In these slum areas there is no heat, no sanitation, and water for hundreds of families may come from a single pump. Although, according to law, all Turkish children must attend at least grade school, many of the "gichiconda" youngsters don't: the girls are kept home to take care of their younger brothers and sisters, and the boys start to work, often at age six, in dank, sunless sweatshops that turn out many of the souvenirs tourists buy in Istanbul's covered market.

All of this would lead most experts to conclude that Istanbul as a nightmare of street crime and juvenile delinquency. It isn't. In fact, there is almost no crime involving teenagers in Turkey. Street fights are usually caused by political, religious or ethnic hatreds and are initiated most often by university students, not young teenagers. No one in the Istanbul police department had ever even heard of a gang war. One high official who had been sent to the United States for police training thought that most of what he had been taught about juvenile mugging, mayhem and murder was quite irrelevant. He also thought that *West Side Story,* which he had seen one evening on Turkish television, was "peculiar." "That's not the kind of juvenile problem we have here," he said. "Children stay at home . . . it's adults who cause the riots between the Greeks and the Turks, the Armenians and the Russians."

Without realizing it he had put his finger on the real difference between Turkish teenagers and those in many other parts of the world. They did, indeed, stay "at home," even when they were working in an Istanbul factory.

Turkey is still basically organized on a village system. Whole groups of families leave the village to seek work and better opportunities in the large cities. But they try to stay together, building their temporary huts in one area—much like the settlers who came to the American West and placed their covered wagons in a circle. The American settlers were trying to protect themselves against strangers: the Indians. The Turkish villagers are also trying to protect themselves against strangers: anyone from a village more than fifty miles from the one where they were born and grew up.

So the groups of villagers who migrate to the city become an extended family; every adult is responsible for every child in the group. The children are taught early in life to obey the adults they know, and some they don't know but who speak with the same accent or dialect as their parents, uncles and cousins. It is not at all uncommon to see a man approach a group of young boys loitering at a street corner and ask sternly: "What are you doing here? Why are you not working? Or in school? Or at home?" If the children don't have a good reason for being where they are, they usually scatter quickly. If three or four youngsters get into a fight on a street, some adult usually pulls them apart and may box the ears of the oldest and strongest, telling him to be ashamed of himself.

It actually should not come as news to those who are concerned about the wild children of the urban ghettos that extended families or close-knit neighborhood groups can be very effective in curbing juvenile crime. When families were close and family associations, known as Tongs, were very influential in Chinese areas of many large cities in the United Sates, there were no wild children in the streets. As Chinese communities in cities like New York and San Francisco grew and children and adults adopted non-Chinese customs and values, the family and family association system began to break down. Now our various Chinatowns are as crime-ridden as most other ghetto areas.

Even in China itself gangs of wild children roamed the streets when the Communist government, in an effort to establish the total authority of the central government, started to remove youngsters from their homes and villages to organize them into Red Guard units. It did not take very long before these bands of teenagers were sneering at their elders, beating up their teachers, vandalizing schools, museums and stores and generally making life very unpleasant for almost all Chinese adults. The government realized, after allowing this to go on for a while, that a mistake had been made. The Red Guard units were dissolved or firm adult control was established over them. Most China watchers now believe that the authority of the family is coming back—nothing else seems to have worked as well in keeping down the juvenile delinquency rate.

In America, almost two decades ago, urbanologist Jane Jacobs, in a book called *Death and Life of Great American Cities,* warned against breaking up city neighborhoods through large urban renewal programs because, she predicted, adult and youth street crimes would go up as a neighborhood's responsible adults were scattered throughout a city. Unfortunately, she proved to be quite right. As the bulldozers moved in to mow down established, if somewhat dilapidated, streets, and huge new housing projects rose on these sites, the crime rate, particularly the juvenile crime rate, doubled and tripled.

This is not only true in the United States but in Europe as well. Glasgow, Scotland, has some of the worst slums of any city in a developed country. The government, in an attempt to improve the lives of its citizens, built large new towns (housing developments with stores, schools, libraries, movie theaters) on the outskirts of Glasgow. The juvenile delinquency rate in these newly developed areas is even higher than it is in the inner city. "Nobody knows anybody around here; it's all so impersonal," one community worker, trying to organize soccer teams and other activities for bored and resentful teenagers, said. "In Glasgow, the troublemakers were known in their neighborhoods. Pubs made sure that they didn't serve alcohol to anyone who was underage. Here we really have no idea who is causing our problems, and the people in the pubs are not nearly as careful to check out how old some of their customers are. So not only are we getting a lot of troublemaking kids, we are getting drunken, troublemaking kids."

In the United States, a report funded by a huge grant from the Carnegie Foundation and published in 1977 suggested that crime could be cut down by improving neighborhood organization and family life. Specific ways of doing this were proposed, but since all of it would cost a great deal of money, nothing has been done about most of the recommendations.

And again, we are not alone. Juvenile crime in the cities of Europe, Asia and Africa has brought about a great deal of hand-wringing, and in the developed societies, a great deal of report writing. But to date no one has really come up with enough money to get at basic changes in the direction of city planning to eliminate the destruction of neighborhoods. Meanwhile, the juvenile gangs get younger. Once they were largely made up of older teenagers, but now there are many made up of grade school and junior high school boys and girls. As city blight spreads, so do the gangs. And as the gangs grow more menacing, people stay at home at night because they are afraid to go out into the streets. As the streets empty out, the wild children take over.

Since the old cities seem to have so many problems, a logical idea might be to start some brand new ones, built to eliminate some of those problems before they even start. A few rulers and planners have actually attempted just that. Let's see what the results are.

3

KINDS OF CITIES
(Some examples)

14

Divided Cities

We have a simple message from this movement for peace.

We want to live and love and build a just and peaceful society.

We want for our children, as we want for ourselves, our lives at home, at work and at play, to be lives of joy and peace.

We recognize that to build such a life demands of all of us dedication, hard work and courage.

We recognize that every bullet fired and every exploding bomb makes that work more difficult.

We reject the use of the bomb and the bullet and all the techniques of violence.

We dedicate ourselves to working with our neighbors, near and far, day in and day out, to building that peaceful society in which the tragedies we have known are a bad memory and a continuing warning.

> Declaration of the Peace People, Belfast, Northern Ireland, October 16, 1976

The very frictions of this place keep us thinking about the world and what we want done with it.

> A West Berlin University Professor

Beirut is dead. . . it was a great city once, but now it's dead.

> A Lebanese banker explaining why his bank's headquarters had been

moved from Beirut, Lebanon to
Aman, Jordan

"Shoot Betty." The graffiti were sprayed in red, dripping
paint on walls of abandoned houses near the center of
Belfast, the embattled capital of Ulster, Northern Ireland.
They are the only spots of color in a cityscape of dark gray
and dirty brown. A cloud of smog hung over Belfast and the
ground was covered with snow, sleet and coal dust, known
locally as "black ice."

The street, formerly a busy commercial area, was de-
serted except for patroling jeeps with British soldiers who
carried their machine guns in plain sight. Both sides of the
street were bordered by twelve-foot-high structures topped
with several feet of barbed wire that looked like two Berlin
walls facing each other with a no-man's-land in between.

During the last week of 1976, it was a coldly terrifying place, a city under siege different from the usual war
zones in that there were no battle lines. A bomb could go
off in any innocent location: a beauty parlor, a flower shop,
a pub. The only large hotel in town had been bombed
twenty times and was closed.

Betty Williams, sitting in front of a gas fire grate in
her small living room in the Catholic section of the city,
divided by bloody warfare between Catholics and Protestants, was obviously tense. No wonder: those blood-red
graffiti were aimed directly at her. Of course, she had been
threatened repeatedly, over the phone and through the
mails, and in Belfast such threats were to be taken seriously.
But no, she wouldn't accept police protection. "An armed
guard in front of my house would be in terrible danger. I
don't want anyone killed on my account." And no, she
didn't want to install "those magical gadgets" the police
were always recommending to secure her doors and windows. "If anyone wants to get me, nothing can protect me,"
she insisted. "I can't let fear paralyze me. That's what's
been wrong with all of us here, for generations. Fear is

what the gunmen are counting on; it's what has made the rule by gun and bomb possible. If we want peace, we can't let fear take over our lives. I don't want to be a bloody martyr. Who does? I love life, but we've declared war on war . . . and at this time, in this place, that's a wee bit risky."

No one meeting Betty Williams for the first time under ordinary circumstances would think of her as a heroine. She's a big, strong, large-boned woman with a toothy Jimmy Carter smile. Her normal greeting is a bear hug. Her normal tone of voice is loud. She can swear like a sailor. (Her husband is a merchant seaman away from home six months at a time.) She admits freely that pacifism doesn't come easily to her. "When I'm mad, I want to screech and kick," she says. Her sweater is often baggy, her eye-shadow electric blue, her mascara runny. She cries easily.

But Betty Williams, coping with all the pressures on her and occasionally clutching a gin and tonic to ward off anxiety and fatigue, is a truly heroic woman. And so, in a different way, is Mairead Corrigan, whom Betty might never have met had they not lived in bitterly divided Belfast, and who, because of a terrible accident in August of 1976, became her partner in the Ulster Peace Movement.

Mairead Corrigan is tiny, soft and gentle. Even in blue jeans, she looks as delicate and elegant as a piece of Irish lace. Where Betty is worldly, Mairead is devoutly religious and steeped in the literature of the international peace movement. When Betty swears, Mairead quotes accurately and easily from Tolstoy, Ghandi and Martin Luther King. As one reporter who has known both women for a long time put it: "They are in a way, mirror images of each other. Together, they represent the ideal Irish woman: tough but gentle, earthy but spiritual, accustomed to violence, yet appalled by it. That's why they have caught the imagination of the world and why they might just bring a measure of peace to this terrorized city."

There's another, more profound reason why Betty and Mairead have become known throughout the world and why, in 1977, they won the Nobel Peace Prize. They are fulfilling a deep psychological need is most of us to find new heroes now that the traditional variety—the man with the sword and the gun—is seen by many of us as someone who endangers human life, rather than protects it. In the cold winter months of 1976 and 1977, Betty's and Mairead's lives were in danger because, in a bitterly divided city, they were peacemakers rather than warriors. They were in jeopardy because they wanted to bridge gaps instead of defending fixed positions. And there's nothing as dangerous as a fixed position in a divided city.

It was a terrible, senseless incident of urban violence that first brought Betty and Mairead together. On August 10th, 1976, in Catholic Andersontown, a few blocks from Betty's small house, an Irish Republican Army getaway car, the driver shot through the heart by a British soldier whom he had attacked, jumped the curb and crushed to death three young children, aged eight years, two years and six weeks. Their mother, Mairead Corrigan's sister, was critically injured. At the funeral home, Mairead saw her eight-year-old niece still holding the dead baby. "Something inside me exploded," she told a reporter. So, with her brother, Jack, the father of the children, she went to the local TV station to denounce the Irish Republican Army, the first Catholic woman in Ulster to date to challenge the gunmen.

The picture of the beautiful young woman, shaking with rage and grief, superimposed on the image of the bloodstained sidewalk and the crushed tricycle, had a powerful effect. The station's switchboard lit up with calls from other Ulster citizens asking what they could do to stop the bloodshed. It is not generally known (because Mairead doesn't mention it) but after the broadcast, she went to the home of the dead IRA driver to comfort his mother and to bring her flowers.

Betty Williams had seen the slaughter. She has not forgotten it to this day. "If I let myself think about those wee children and their mother, I just want to stand in a corner and scream," she said recently. Instead, she took drastic action. She went home, sat down at her battered second-hand typewriter and composed a peace petition. Then she walked up and down the streets of Andersontown banging on doors and asking anyone who answered to sign her petition and to join her in a peace rally the following Saturday. Since many of the strangers who answered those doors could be expected to be members of the Irish Republican Army, her actions required a special kind of courage. But many of those to whom she spoke, signed. Her one-woman crusade was picked up by a Belfast newspaper. Mairead read about it and called her on the telephone. The People's Peace Movement was born.

The first rally drew a small crowd, mostly frightened women. The next rally drew more. The third rally turned into a peace march that surprised everyone. Catholic women from the Falls and Andersontown marched across the fortified dividing line that separated them from their Protestant sisters on Shankill, who greeted them like long lost friends. Women who had lived only a few blocks apart but who had never spoken to each other except with curses, now hugged, embraced and cried on each other's shoulders. Then they walked together through the walled no-man's-land, singing: "We Shall Overcome." (Identified by one Shankill resident as "a fine old song.") At one point, the police estimated the crowd of marchers at more than twenty thousand. No rally of that size had ever been held in Belfast before for *any* reason.

The Peace People have long since ceased to be just local Belfast news. Their activities have been covered by newspapers and magazines throughout the world. Betty and Mairead have won the Nobel Peace Prize. They have been received by the President of the United States and other important political figures. They have won decorations from the Pope and from Queen Elizabeth of England. In 1978, they spoke before the United Nations.

Obviously, Betty and Mairead had hit a deep wellspring

among an urban population that was tired of violence, tired of gunmen, tired of bombs and fires and death. Because of the "Peace People" and others like them it's possible that divided Belfast is healing sufficiently to become a viable city again.

The same, unfortunately, is not true of other divided cities. Beirut has been almost totally destroyed in the battle between Catholics and Mohammedans, conservatives and revolutionaries. The bank of the businessman who called the city "dead" was not the only commercial organization to move out. Beirut was once a headquarters for the international gold market. The city had the best harbor in the Middle East, with cargo and passenger ships coming and going every day. That harbor was destroyed. Even the smuggling boats, once regular visitors, have abandoned Beirut for safer waters. (Naples seems to be their new port of call.) Anyone with enough money and influence to leave has left. Those who remain in bombed-out, burned-out homes have nowhere else to go and no money to get anywhere, even if they could find a new home. A sad, homesick peddler who now lives in Cairo tells of the good old days when he owned a fleet of taxicabs in Beirut. "We had such a beautiful city," he says. "Nowhere did the Mediterranean look bluer and cleaner than from our beaches. We could look up from the sparkling water to the snow-covered mountains that rose above our city. There were green trees, flowers and birds everywhere. Now there's nothing left. They've even burned down the trees, and the birds had enough sense not to stay . . . as I did." Is there a chance that he may go back home? "I dream about it," he said, "but there's no real hope. We were always a divided city. But somehow Christians and Moslems managed to live in some kind of precarious peace. The existence of our city depended on this peace. But now it's broken, and it's almost impossible to restore. There's no common ground between the two factions. They have nothing to talk about. And there's no city left to fight over . . . but they keep on fighting any-way."

Berlin, Germany, is a different kind of divided city. There are no guns or bombs. But an impenetrable wall divides the East from the West, separating families and lifelong friends. The wall has been there for so long now (since 1961) that a whole generation of teenagers has grown up knowing only half of the city.

Berlin, in the 1920s and early '30s, before the Nazis took over, was a very special place. It was a magnet for some of the best writers, composers, artists and architects from all over the world. The most spectacular modern theater, the most controversial art exhibits, the best con-certs could be found in Berlin. English writers like poet W. H. Auden and novelist Christopher Isherwood, who wrote the book *Berlin Stories* (on which the motion picture *Cabaret* was based), celebrated the open and free life of the city. The locals talked about a mysterious quality, "Berliner Luft" (which means, literally, "Berlin air"), that to them summed up the special quality of the city. Since the air in Berlin was as polluted as that in other great cities, they actually were talking about a quality of life and a free-dom that artists, writers and composers enjoyed in Berlin.

Even the coming of the Nazis did not totally alter the special feelings Berliners had about themselves. The Nazis were less successful in Berlin than in most other German urban areas. Hitler got fewer votes in Berlin during the 1933 election that brought him to power than he did in any other large German city. Before the beginning of World War II, Berliners still joked about "the little man with the moustache." He spoke there rarely, because he found that he did not receive the enthusiastic response he got in Munich or Leipzig or Frankfurt. Berlin had kept its skep-ticism as well as its sense of humor. After 1941, jokes about the government became too dangerous. One could be sent to a concentration camp, or even be executed, for making fun of Hitler or any of his cohorts. But those who remained in the city through thick and thin, through hunger and fear and constant bombings still talk about the special grace under pressure of the Berliners.

At the end of World War II, Germany was split in two, and Berlin itself was divided into an East and a West sector. The city was surrounded by territory given to East Germany, but half of the city was considered to be a part of West Germany: a tiny embattled island of freedom in a sea of Communism and repression. It was difficult to live in West Berlin, especially after the East German government, with strong encouragement from the Russians, cut off all ground transportation, leaving West Berlin without an access to the outside world. The United States for months supplied the city's needs, which included not only food and medicine, but also fuel and building materials, by air.

In spite of these hardships, old Berliners, including many famous artists, writers and musicians, returned. The city began rebuilding its bomb-damaged areas relatively quickly. Where formerly one of the world's greatest zoos, the Tiergarten, had been located, a new and beautiful housing development was built. The Hansaviertel was the result of an international archectural competition and boasts of buildings by some of the world's greatest architects: Van der Rohe, Saaranin and Aalto. Concert halls and theaters were rebuilt even before commerce and industry came back. There were innumerable new libraries, a new first-rate university, and at one point, twenty-three thriving daily newspapers.

If West Berlin was a conspicuous economic and cultural success, East Germany and East Berlin were not. So, at first slowly and then in a rapidly increasing flood, East Germans and East Berliners used the subway and the trains that connected the two parts of the city to remove themselves and their families to the freer and more prosperous West. The most educated and most skilled came first, and soon East Germany was experiencing a brain drain of unprecedented proportions.

On a bright Sunday morning, August 13th, 1961, Berliners woke up to the stunned realization that their politically-divided city was now physically divided as well: the East Germans, with the help of Russian tanks and heavy construction equipment, had built an all but impregnable wall between the two halves. The wall was made of rubble and connected bombed-out buildings. Windows and doors in those buildings had been closed tight with bricks and mortar. The wall was topped with about four feet of ugly, rusty barbed wire and bits of broken glass and steel. During the night, a few East Berliners had noticed the commotion near their homes and quickly crossed over to West Berlin, some taking only a change of clothing along. They realized that they might never have another chance to escape to the West—and they were right.

As the wall grew higher and thicker, some young Germans still tried to cross by land or to swim across the Spree, the river that runs through the middle of Berlin. But East German policemen and Russian soldiers with submachine guns were guarding these exits. No one really knows how many people have been killed trying to escape, but since August 13th, 1961, very few have managed to get out of East Berlin.

One of the few who did make it, and who, for a brief time became a world celebrity, was seventeen-year-old Christel Welsch, a tiny, blue-eyed, entrancingly pretty East Berliner. With thirteen other young people, plus her mother, she managed to kidnap a passenger steamer (meant for more than five hundred people) and run it across the River Spree from the East Sector of Berlin to the West. First, she says, she tried to steal a smaller boat. She didn't make it. Then her boyfriend told her that he knew one of the captains of the East German Spree Excursion Line. The captain liked Kümmel, a particularly potent German alcoholic beverage, and pretty women. They felt that if Christel arrived on board with a bottle after the boat had docked for the night, she would be welcomed with open arms. He turned out to be right.

While Christel encouraged the captain to drink up, her mother and several friends (one carrying an eight-month-old baby) waited in the high grass for a signal that the captain was out of commission for the night. "We figured we'd also carry one of the most unlikely objects anyone trying to escape from East Berlin would have on them," Christel told reporters a few days after her escape. "We decided that a bowl of vanilla pudding with a pitcher of strawberry sauce would certainly look innocent. If we were stopped by a soldier or by the border police, we'd just say we were carrying the sloppy mess to a friend's house for a birthday party. We also wrapped the baby in colored paper like a present, and hoped it wouldn't cry."

They made it across the river under fire from Russian gun boats. "I was so scared, I ate the whole pudding," Christel said. After her escape and the brief fame that her escapade brought her, she settled in a street on the West side of the wall, only a few blocks from her former home. When last heard from, she had married the friend who had told her about the Spree boat captain and was working as a nurses' aide in one of Berlin's many large hospitals. She had received several offers for modeling jobs, personal appearances and other more glamorous activities from England, France and even America right after her well-publicized escape. But she decided that she did not want to leave her hometown. "I am a Berliner," she said, unconsciously echoing President John F. Kennedy, who was to make that statement a year later, standing before the Berlin City Hall to let the Berliners know that the United States government would not allow their free city to be swallowed up by East Germany.

Another young Berliner was not so successful. Peter Fechter, an eighteen-year-old construction worker, tried to escape from East Berlin on August 18, 1961, by climbing a relatively unprotected section of the ten foot high wall near "Checkpoint Charlie," where foreigners were allowed to cross over from East to West. He was sighted by a German border guard, shot and left to die in no-man's-land.

His screams attracted a crowd of West Berliners, including many students from the Free University. For a while it looked as if a confrontation was inevitable, which might bring about the destruction of the fragile peace between the two Germanys. The students, listening to the pathetic cries of Peter Fechter, armed themselves with sticks, stones, gasoline-filled bottle bombs and started to storm the wall. But a solid line of West German policemen held back the crowd. The young officers looked white and sick, but they firmly kept back the students. "It won't help for you to attack. It won't help, go home," they insisted. "If you move against them, they will shoot. Someone on your side will shoot back. That is the way wars start."

For a while, Berlin's energetic and brilliant young Mayor, Willy Brandt, joined the police in pleading with the crowds. Standing on a flatbed truck, tears in his eyes, he told the students that the survival of the city might depend on remaining calm. Brandt, who many years later, as Chancellor of West Germany, would win the Nobel Peace Prize, was as staunchly anti-Communist as he had been anti-Nazi. (A native Berliner, he had fought in the Norwegian underground against the German army during World War II.) He finally persuaded the crowd to leave. Peter Fechter died, and East German border guards dragged his lifeless body back to East Berlin. The incident served as a warning to others in the East who might try to scale the Berlin wall. Fewer and fewer attempted to flee into West Berlin. But, to this day, an occasional brave and determined refugee still makes it.

Berlin is continuing to exist as a divided city. There is no violence between the two halves. On both sides of the wall, Germans and foreigners have accepted the inevitable, even though many have little hope of ever seeing family and friends on the opposite side again. West Berlin has never quite regained its old sparkle. The city looks fairly prosperous, but the population is getting older. Few young people want to settle there even though the German government provides cost of living allowances and tax breaks to residents of West Berlin. They find they have the feeling of being locked in, stifled. Even without the kind of urban violence that has destroyed Beirut, and may still destroy Belfast, Berlin is slowly deteriorating into a gray, slightly elderly city. There's still good theater and good music, but building has slowed down, industry is moving away, and it becomes increasingly evident that, without outside help, West and East Berlin would not be able to withstand the problems brought about by the division. There are still Berliners on both sides of the wall who, like the now almost middle-aged Christel Welsch, won't leave. "I won't go until they throw me out," Christel said in a recent interview. "And then, I'll be on the very last train to leave my city."

15

Instant Cities

The seat of the Turkish state is Angora.

> From the law setting up the modern
> Turkish state, passed by the first
> Grand National Assembly. April 16,
> 1923

It may be that a city is simply an Act of God, rather
than an act of architecture. . . .

> Ada Louise Huxtable in a *New York
> Times* article, Nov. 19, 1978

There are cities that are settled by a hardy few who have
somehow found the right place for a city to be, and over the
decades and centuries these cities thrive. There are other
cities settled, usually for monetary gain or out of just plain
greed, by large industries, governments or private individuals who want to get rich quickly and then leave. The
purpose of these cities is usually a temporary one, such as
a gold rush, or more recently, the discovery of oil or natural
gas. Once the original reason for the city has either not
materialized or has been exhausted, these cities vanish or
deteriorate. Then there are cities that seem to have been
settled for no practical reason, but that somehow manage
to survive the ages. Within fairly recent times, another kind
of city has appeared in various countries, the instant city.

The instant city usually comes into existence because
a government or single ruler has decided that "X" marks the
spot where a city is needed, not five or ten years from now,

but next year, or preferably, next month. Almost all instant cities have built-in problems. Let's look at one example: Ankara, Turkey.

Unlike Istanbul, which grew slowly through the ages, involving many new ethnic groups and races, and which is situated on an almost ideal site for beauty as well as for trade and commerce, Ankara grew from a small village on a mountain plateau with more goats than people into the capital of Turkey within a few years. The reason for this was the wish of one man, Kemal Mustafa, better known as Ataturk or father of Turkey.

The legend is that when Ataturk was not yet in power but trying to escape with his life from the Ottoman rulers of Turkey, the hardy peasants and goat herders of the small town on the Anatolian plateau, Angora (after the wool produced by the goats), decided to hide him and keep him safe. When he left, he promised that he would come back after defeating the evil Ottoman rulers and make Angora the capital of a bright, prosperous new Turkey. That's the legend. The truth is probably less picturesque and a little more practical.

When Ataturk took over the government of his country, he realized that its population centers, which bordered the various oceans and bodies of water within and surrounding Turkey, were crowded and overpopulated. On the other hand, the Anatolian plateau was barren, desolate and inaccessible, and had hardly any population. With one-third of his country overcrowded and the other two-thirds virtually uninhabited desert land, Ataturk decided that the population would have to be shifted in some fundamental way in order to take advantage of all the land. One method to do this would be to put the center of the new country in the center of the land. So, he moved the capital from Istanbul on the ocean to Angora (of which, indeed, he may have had some fond memories) and renamed the new town Ankara.

Everything about Ankara, except a tiny settlement

called "The Fortress," is less than seventy-five years old. In fact, much is less than twenty-five years old. Where goats once tried to survive on the few miserable weeds and scruffy bushes that managed to outlast the bone-dry summers and freezing winters, huge government office complexes, sky-scraper apartment houses, schools and hospitals, hotels and other distinctly urban construction projects rise like illustra-tions from the latest American architectural magazine. Within decades Ankara has grown from a town of a few thousand to a city of over five hundred thousand and is growing still.

But there are many problems that must be solved or Ankara may, within the next few hundred years, shrink as fast as it grew in the past few decades. For instance, there is not enough water, nor has anyone yet found a method of obtaining this vital necessity for the growing city. Most of Ankara's water comes from a small river or is gathered from a few annual rainstorms. It is kept in a reservoir out-side the city. But there never was enough water, even when Ankara was relatively small, and adding rainwater to the existing supply is not really solving the problem. As the summer days and nights grow longer and hotter, the water level in the reservoir drops. It has become a favorite sport for Ankara citizens to have a Sunday picnic out at the reservoir (the only body of fresh water within hundreds of square miles.) They watch the water level drop from week to week, and make bets on the day when there will be no water at all. This has not yet happened, but those who watch Ankara's growth carefully fear that the time is not far off when it might.

Meanwhile, the city has some stringent water-saving policies. During the summer months all city water is turned off for hours at a time. As the water shortage inevitably grows in August, the water is only turned on for an hour or so a day, sometimes in the middle of the night. Everyone in Ankara watches the newspapers and listens to the radio, which give daily "water hours." If the water runs from two

Transportation

Above: Sometimes, in a rush-hour crowd, walking still gets you from here to there fastest.

Right: Workers transport hundreds of pounds of stones by cart in India. Mule carts are still only for the moderately well-to-do. Elephants and automobiles are for the very rich.

Right: Millions of people want to use planes to get from one city to another as quickly as possible, but nobody likes to have an airport near his or her home. In Hong Kong, where there is little space, the airport is almost in the middle of the city, and planes sometimes look as if they were about to land on one's head.

Above: In hot Jerusalem, this man is lucky to have a mule to climb the hills, instead of having to use his feet.

Right: In the least industrial cities of the world, people are the principal means of carrying goods from one place to another. This man in Katmandu, Nepal, is carrying at least two hundred pounds of rice on his shoulders.

Right: Bikes are still the most common
form of city transportation in most of the
world. They might even become popular
in American cities as the price of gasoline
rises. These men are trying to get to work
during the morning rush hour in New
Delhi.

Below: Hong Kong, one of the most
densely populated cities in the world, has
to transport so many people that even the
trams are double-decked.

Below right: Japanese bullet trains are so
fast that it is impossible, even with a
high-speed camera, to get a picture that
is anything but a blur. They are also clean,
comfortable and almost invariably on time.

to three in the morning, everybody turns on an alarm, gets up, and fills all available containers with the precious liquid, which will have to last until the next "water hours."

Ataturk wanted his city to be modern and beautiful. He admired, as much as any American city planner, such conveniences as bathrooms with flush toilets and hot and cold running showers. Some of Ankara's high-rise buildings have swimming pools (usually on the roof). The government buildings constructed in recent years have air-conditioning equipment. All of these new, modern constructions require water in order to function, but water is simply not available much of the time.

Modern Ankara buildings also have central heat installations for the winter. But the railroad line that connects the capital city with the coal mining areas in the rest of the country does not have a wide enough roadbed nor enough tracks to carry sufficient coal to keep all those buildings warm. So, in some of Ankara's most luxurious and expensive apartments, there are small coal and oil stoves that supply the only heat on a freezing winter night. The central heating system probably quit in November when the supply of coal ran out.

Since Ankara is on a mountain plateau, very few fruits and vegetables, and no grain or rice is grown nearby. Few animals (except the Angora goats that provide much better wool than meat) can survive on the land.

There are, of course, no fish. The few chickens that manage to make it to adulthood are so tough and scrawny that many foreigners feel they need a long vacation on a Kansas farm before meeting their end on some rich family's dinner table. Poor Ankara residents can't afford chicken— on Sunday or any other day.

But even for the rich, the food supply in the city is often meager. There are no signs of obvious hunger or even serious malnutrition, because the Turkish government manages to keep enough food coming into the city and controls the prices on necessities ruthlessly, to make sure that no one starves. But there are days when cabbage, powdered milk and potatoes are available in the market stalls and little else anywhere, except in the very expensive grocery stores that stock canned goods. Frozen food is just beginning to make its appearance in Turkish markets, and, of course, in the summer there may not be enough electricity to keep the freezers running in Ankara.

Then there is the problem of jobs. Ankara is strictly a one industry town, and the industry is government. Almost anyone who has a job works for the government, works for someone else who works for the government, or works in a service industry that supplies the needs of government workers. This was not what Ataturk had in mind when he located this capital on that mountain plateau. He dreamed of a city that would attract major industries, not only from the rest of Turkey, but from other lands. But Ankara is simply too remote from sources of raw materials to become a viable industrial center.

Many years after Ataturk's death, another Turkish ruler with high ambitions for Ankara decided that a sugar factory for the region would be a good first step towards industrialization. The sugar factory (one of the more luxurious factory buildings in the Middle East) was constructed; ribbons were cut with great ceremony, and sugar production was slated to begin. There was one great difficulty, however, which might have been foreseen. The same railroads that could not bring enough coal into the city to keep it warm in the winter, could not bring in enough sugar beets to keep the factory humming throughout the year. The same electrical failures that plagued apartment buildings and government offices, of course, also disrupted factory production. And then there were not enough freight cars or trucks, or highways for the trucks to use, to get the sugar out of Ankara even if it might have been produced in quantity. So, after a year or so, the sugar factory was given a new role: it was turned over to the United Nations, which started, in cooperation with the Turkish government, an architectural, engineering and city planning school to train students from the entire Middle East not to repeat the same kinds of mistakes that were made when Ankara was planned.

On a recent visit, in the middle of a hot summer day, there were still families watching the water level drop . . . only this time they were joined by students who were dreaming of schemes to increase the water supply so that Ankara would not turn from an instant city into an instant disaster. Perhaps, one of them may find such a scheme. In that case, Ankara will, of course, continue to grow (all government cities do) and may some day fulfill the dreams that Ataturk dreamed when he ordered its creation.

There are similar instant cities with some of Ankara's problems and a few unique ones of their own. Brasilia was founded for many of the same reasons that prompted the construction of Ankara: a new city in the center of a country whose population was concentrated on the edges. It too abounds in modern skyscrapers and hotels. It's principal industry is also government. And it too suffers from lack of water, electricity, employment opportunities and social services to support the many poor who come there hoping to find a better life.

Other instant cities seem to contain fewer ingredients for their own future demise, but they also tend to be places in which it is not very pleasant to live because they have none of the amenities that make life in a city attractive. There is Bonn, West Germany, for instance. Bonn, until the end of World War II, was a sleepy little university town, principally known as the birthplace of Ludwig van Beethoven. An annual Beethoven festival was held in one of the university's large halls. Tourists came to listen to the music and drink the wonderful white wines from the grapes that grew in the hills surrounding the town and to take a boat along the Rhine River, which borders the town. A prime attraction was Lorelei Rock, which was pointed out by guides in many languages, on which the seductress was supposed to have lured her admirers to their death, until

Lorelei was banned by Hitler, who discovered that the man who had written the poem was a Jew, Heinrich Heine.

It never occurred to anyone, not even the president of the town's booster club, to consider Bonn a major German city, much less to regard it as a potential capital. But since Bonn had few military installations (Cologne, across the river was an important target), it managed to survive World War II bombings in much better shape than most other urban areas.

When the first West German government was selected, the question of a capital for the country was carefully discussed. Berlin, the traditional capital, was out of the question. It had been divided into several sectors and, what's more, was situated in the middle of what was now a new and hostile country: East Germany.

The first Chancellor of Germany was an elderly man who had been a professor at the University of Bonn: Konrad Adenauer. He liked Bonn and didn't want to move, many Germans say today. So he, the story goes, suggested that Bonn would make as good a capital as any other city . . . a few new buildings, a few highways connecting the little town with the rest of Germany would, of course, be needed. But the location was not only pretty but central. All the foreign diplomats would enjoy the lovely view of the Rhine, the good music and excellent local wines. Adenauer's points seemed reasonable: Bonn became the new capital of West Germany. The sleepy university town was on its way to becoming an instant metropolis.

Bonn does not have the built-in geographical disadvantages of either Ankara or Brasilia. There is plenty of water, electricity, more jobs than people to fill them, since major industrial cities are within easy commuting distance, and all the supporting services like hospitals, schools and social agencies that anyone might need. The problem is that Bonn has lost in charm and interest what it has gained in wealth and power. Foreign journalists covering Europe dread being sent to Bonn. The universal judgment is that it's boring and expensive. The annual Beethoven Festival now takes place in a huge, newly built "Beethoven Halle," and tickets have become so expensive that few local residents can afford them. Besides, they complain, the acoustics are terrible. The University is still one of the foremost in Europe, but it's no longer a place of peace and beauty. It's at the center of an unplanned megalopolis. Land values around Bonn have risen astronomically, so that many of the wine growers are selling their land, taking their millions in profit, and retiring to sleepy little mountain towns in Switzerland, which, to them, still have the charm that Bonn lost when it became an instant city.

In recent years the German government has begun to have serious second thoughts about the largely unplanned growth of Bonn, which has now extended its borders to another formerly sleepy little tourist resort called Bad Godesberg. Air pollution, water pollution, traffic jams, substandard housing at ruinous prices, land speculation—all these problems are ever-present. Lorelei is back on her rock. She was rehabilitated after Hitler's demise, but there are few tourists to listen to the sad story of suitors lured to their death. Tourists tend to go to areas where they can find peace and beauty. Little of that is left in Bonn or Bad Godesberg.

There are those who believe that a city, like a civilization, takes time to grow and develop. Instant cities tend to be like instant foods: profitable, but not very appetizing or nourishing. We may reach a time in the life of our planet when we are able to plan a city today and start to build it tomorrow without losing the qualities that make urban life attractive to most of us. So far, however, no one seems to have managed to devise such a plan.

16

New Towns

. . . a town is not the result of a design program; it is the reflection of a way of life.

Bernard Rudofsky, *Streets for People*

Another way governments have tried to cope with over-crowded urban areas is to design and build miniature instant cities, usually called "New Towns." Most of the time these are intensely modern in design, carefully planned by sociologists, social anthropologists, economists, an occasional psychiatrist and a myriad of architects and engineers. Also, the people who live in them are apt to hate them. This seems to be, with a few minor exceptions, almost universally true, whether the New Town is located on the outskirts of Paris, a few miles from Stockholm, in the vicinity of Glasgow, in the bombed-out center of West Berlin, or in the exurban outskirts of Washington, D.C.

This is what noted architectural and urban design critic, Ada Louise Huxtable, had to say in an article called appropriately enough, "Cold Comfort: The New French Towns," in the November 19, 1978, issue of the *New York Times Magazine.* "The distance from Paris to Creteil (one of the New Towns) is about five miles, but it may as well be a trip to the moon. Paris is the product of the rational refinements of centuries of a magnificent architectural and urban tradition. But this tradition finds no reflection in the Paris region's new towns. Parisian neighborhoods combine housing, shops, offices, administration, entertainment and the arts in a vital, organic mix. Creteil's residential neighbor-

hoods . . . are designed by several architects to avoid
monotony, but unlike Paris's natural variety, their differences are cosmic. . . .

"Paris's elegant and sophisticated architecture, which
has evolved slowly through centuries of French academic
style, make it the most beautiful and urbane city in the
world. In Creteil, the intimate Parisian streetscape has given
way to a surreal plazascape with towers in the center city,
and an abstract alienating pattern of horizontal and undulat-
ing stripes, replacing the comfortable, familiar measure of
streets, doors and windows."

A Berlin taxi driver who had just moved into a modern,
carefully planned apartment in the Hansaviertel, built in the
bombed-out center of the city after a widely publicized international design competition, had never heard of Ada Louise
Huxtable, French (or German) academic style, or alienating
patterns. But he made the same point that she did when he
commented: "This isn't Berlin . . . it's a movie set. Whoever thought this one up had seen too many flicks about the
twenty-first century and space ships that land on Venus."

Not only did he criticize the design, which he found
cold, uncomfortable and generally "peculiar," the place
simply did not suit either his own or his family's lifestyle.
"We used to live in an old, rundown, two-story house in the
Moabiet" (a section of Berlin a little like the street on which
Archie Bunker lives in Queens, New York), he said. "They
condemned the whole street because several bombs had
fallen near enough to shake the foundations of some of the
houses. Of course, it took them more than twenty-years to
discover that . . . but anyway, they told us we had to get
out and they had these great new apartments for us. Well,
the old lady and I took one look at the fifteen-story apartment house they were sending us to, and we knew right
away we were in trouble.

"In the first place, we've got five kids. They love the
elevators. They spend all day riding up and down. That
makes the other tenants mad, and they complain to my wife

who has had to practically lock up the kids. What's more, you can't see them from the twelfth story where we live when they are out playing on the street. Only three of the five are in school yet, so all day long my wife has at least two kids around. At night she's tired and grouchy. It isn't all the new apartment, of course, but that's a lot of it. They just weren't thinking about a working man with a lot of kids when they built the Hansaviertel.

"Then there's not a whole lot for me to do when I get home at night either. As a matter of fact, the only place I like to go is a sort of beer garden someone has set up in the basement. That's illegal, of course, but the police leave the place alone, because one of the cops lives in the Hansaviertel too, and that's the only place *he* wants to go at night.

"They've got all kinds of theaters and concert halls and libraries, but after a hard day in a taxi, who needs that? Maybe the gentlemen architects who planned the place would like to spend their evenings soaking up culture, but I never was interested in that kind of 'elegant' entertainment in the first place. Some of us have suggested that they might want to turn one of those culture places into a bowling alley, but everybody in the city planning office was insulted . . . at least that's the way they acted.

"The rent for the apartment is cheap. The city pays for part of it . . . and we've got all kinds of new gadgets, like a refrigerator with a freezer. But my wife has her sister looking for a place for us in the Moabiet. Perhaps she'll find something before we get a divorce, or the kids drive us nuts, or I lost my temper one evening and break one of those huge glass windows they insist on putting everywhere."

A social worker in one of the New Towns near Glasgow told stories that in many ways were similar to that of the Berlin taxi driver, Kurt, except that the population in her particular instant city was much more disturbed than the wholesome though disgruntled Berlin family.

"This town was built when they condemned some of the worst Glasgow slums," she said. "They brought the people out here, right from their slum environment. Well, perhaps you could take those people out of the slums, but you couldn't take the slum culture out of the people. The place had some of the finest architects and planners working on it, they tell me. As a matter of fact, recently someone showed me a whole pile of English and American architectural magazines, which praise the place to the skies. Some of those planners and some of those editors should have met the people who are living here now, before they judged the town a success."

The New Town near Glasgow also has high-rise buildings with elevators, just like the Hansaviertel. While in the Hansaviertel many of the mothers complain about inaccessible play yards, they take their complaints out on the neighbors, their husbands, and an occasional city official. In the Scottish New Town they are apparently taking out their unhappiness on the children. "The incidence of violence against kids, including small babies, was always high in the Glasgow slums," the social worker said. "Here it's astronomical. The mothers are cooped up with their kids all day, and too many lose control of their emotions and beat the kids unmercifully. Also, everybody realized that there was a lot of alcoholism in the Glasgow slums, so they thought they'd control the situation here by allowing only a few pubs and even fewer liquor stores. Anybody who knows a drunk realizes that that's just a stupid plan. The men, and the women, who want to drink just go off to Glasgow, leaving the kids with whoever will take care of them. Often the men spend their nights in town, leaving their wives alone. We have more broken families here than we did when these same people still lived in those tenements. On the whole, I'd call this place a disaster area."

A group of women, meeting in one of the many laundromats scattered throughout the New Town, tended to agree with the social worker. "I could wash all the clothes once a week," one woman said, "but I come here every day.

It's the only place I can go in this whole town where I can watch the kids and also talk to other people. They've built all kinds of social clubs, libraries and meeting halls in this town, but I feel completely uncomfortable there. All those social workers and teachers who want to try to change me get on my nerves. At least here I can let my hair down . . . or more exactly, keep it up in curlers, without feeling like a slut." And then, echoing Kurt, the taxi driver, she too indicated that the people who had planned the New Town simply did not understand her life style. "This place was put together for swells, elegant ladies with nannies for their kids. They like to play bridge in the afternoon or go to tea parties at the vicar's house," she said. "I like to go out for a beer, or to get some fish and chips. Mainly, I need to get away from the kids. And I don't even know my next door neighbor yet, so I can't ask her to babysit. In Glasgow, I knew everybody in the house . . . but then nobody planned for us to have 'privacy' there. Who needs privacy? I need company."

A young attorney, traveling on a sleek, shiny modern train to his office in Stockholm, Sweden, from a sleek, shiny modern New Town, indicated on the other hand, that he rather liked his living arrangements. The architects and planners who had designed them obviously understood his life syle, the way they did not understand Kurt's or that of the laundromat woman's. His apartment was attractive, relatively affordable, airy and convenient, he said. He enjoyed the many cultural and sports facilities that had been included in the town plan. His young son's day care center seemed to be a model of efficient planning but also showed imaginative concern for the needs of young children. He did not mind the forty-five minutes he spent on the train. He could use the time to organize his work, before and after office hours.

But he, too, admitted that he had a dream. Someday, when his practice had grown to be really prosperous, he would like to buy a cooperative apartment in one of those elegant townhouses, built in the nineteenth century in the center of Stockholm and renovated lovingly and tastefully every twenty years by a series of gifted architects and craftsmen. "Of course, those places are prohibitively expensive," he said, quoting a price that would seem high even to a prospective buyer of real estate on New York's Park Avenue. (Stockholm's real estate prices are exceeded only by those in Tokyo.) "The New Town is great," he said. "But it lacks style and romance. Stockholm, with all those beautiful vaulted bridges and medieval-looking towers, always reminded me of the stories I read in school about King Arthur's court at Camelot. I'd like to enjoy my middle age with a little more Camelot and a little less steel and glass, if that's possible."

The last of the new towns we shall visit in this chapter is not new . . . actually, it's centuries old, and was not meant to be lived in at all. It's a City of the Dead, at the foot of the old Citadel in the center of Cairo, Egypt. There in 1000 acres of graveyards filled with large limestone, alabaster and granite mausoleums live anywhere from 75,000 to 200,000 Egyptians. The government is not sure of the number of families because officials gave up counting years ago. Some of the tombs are the home of one family. Several of the larger ones are shared by several households.

There are grocery stores in tombs, barber shops in tombs and coffee houses in tombs. When families first started moving into the old graveyard, the city officials of Cairo tried to evict them. But they soon found that this was an impossible task. As soon as the police removed one set of residents, another moved in. Cairo has one of the worst housing shortages in the world. Egypt is a very poor country and building new towns, although planning is now underway for several of them, will take many years. Also, much of the country is desert and there is a shortage of livable, buildable land.

The attitude of the Egyptian government towards the tomb dwellers therefore was realistic, humanitarian and sensible. Instead of continuing to evict the people, it was decided to make the tombs as habitable as possible. The city put in electricity and sewers. Bus lines now run through the tomb-lined streets, and at peak traffic hours, policemen direct the crowds of cars, trucks, carts, donkeys and the occasional camel that block the way to all other forms of transportation.

The taxi driver who lives in the City of the Dead drives a very different kind of car from Berlin Kurt's shiny new $15,000 Mercedes. He is the owner of a twenty-year-old Chevrolet, which looks as if only infinite patience and care keep it running at all. But by Egyptian standards, Achmed is as rich a man as Kurt is by German ones. In Egypt, even to own a donkey is a sign that one is a man of property. And unlike Kurt, Achmed likes his particular home. His reasons are interesting because, in a strange way, the tomb community, which looks like the most desperate of slums to most foreign visitors, avoids many of the objections that everyone from Ada Louise Huxtable to the Swedish lawyer have had to instant cities.

Achmed insists that his father was one of the first to move into the City of the Dead. "When we came from the village, after a particularly bad drought, there was simply no place for us to go in Cairo," he said. "My father, my ten-year old brother and I had to look for work. We had no money . . . not even enough for food. Even if we could have found a place to rent, which we couldn't, we would not have been able to pay for it. We were wandering around the streets, sleeping on sidewalks and in the courts of mosques and were constantly being driven away by the police. One day we wandered into this huge graveyard. The tombs were large, looked beautiful and kept out the hot sun in the summer. We later found that they were also very easy to heat in the winter with a small oil stove. So we just moved in.

"When others came from our village, my father told them about our free house, and they moved in next door. Pretty soon somebody opened up a small food store in a tomb. Street after street of tombs filled up with people.

Usually people from the same village moved in next door to each other. There were lots of tombs . . . so we all had a choice of where we wanted to settle. We bought or built a little furniture . . . and with the money we earned, we were able to eat. Of course, in the beginning the police chased us out every once in a while. But we'd leave for a day, and then just move back in. Now the government is very reasonable. They've put in electricity and some water fountains so that our women don't have to walk for miles to get water to cook and wash with. Cairo water is much healthier than the Nile water we used to have in the village, you know. Because I don't pay rent, I was able to save enough money for this taxi. Now I make a very good living for my wife and five sons."

Achmed is visibly proud of himself, and he has a right to that pride. In a country where almost half of the male population is unemployed and where the standard of living is among the lowest in the Arab world, he has done very well. Through initiative, thrift and imagination, he is a businessman—a man of property. Besides, he enjoys driving a taxi and meeting all kinds of people, including the foreign tourists who now visit Egypt in great numbers. He has taught himself to read and write. And with the help of some Peace Corps volunteers who, several years ago, lived in an old house near the City of the Dead, he has learned some English.

His wife is too shy to talk to strangers, but she follows her husband as he shows his foreign guests the living accommodations in his tomb-house and offers a cup of thick, sweet Turkish coffee like any good Egyptian host. "My wife likes it here, too," he says. "There are many people from our village here. When someone needs help, there are always friends . . . and it's important to live where one has friends. Everybody looks after everyone else's kids. My wife wouldn't let Muhemod's kids next door get into any kind of trouble . . . and his wife would make sure that ours didn't get run over by a cart or trampled by a camel. The women do their laundry together. They bake together. The men meet at the coffee house at night. You may think this is strange, but we find this is a good place to live."

Then he looks up at Cairo's ancient city walls and at one of the most beautiful mosques in the Arab world that rises on a hill just above the City of the Dead. "It's beautiful here sometimes," he says. "So many people have lived in Cairo, for so many thousands of years. Here you feel that. You don't at the Hilton." In a place that would seem a symbol of abject misery to most of us, Achmed seems to have found at least some elements of his kind of Camelot.

Of course, this does not mean that conditions in the City of the Dead provide an even remotely acceptable standard of living. As Egypt plans for the future, new and better homes must be found for the tomb dwellers. But there are lessons to be learned from that strange and seemingly impossible cluster of homes. What the tomb dwellers seem to have found, along with a roof over their heads, is a sense of community, a sense of control over their own lives that many of the citizens of the sophisticated, planned New Towns lack. Urban life, at its best, has always given city dwellers these advantages. But usually they took generations to produce. Apparently the inhabitants of the City of the Dead have managed to incorporate some of these human qualities into their homes, even though they lack almost all the facilities most of us would consider necessary to a healthy life.

About ten years ago, a New Haven architect, Gilbert Switzer, was asked to replan and redesign a community for about twenty-five thousand people on the outskirts of Springfield, Massachusetts. The area, formerly inhabited by working class families, first and second generation Poles, Italians and European Jews, was running down fast. The inhabitants had moved into the suburbs, leaving their homes to absentee landlords who bought them for speculation, rented them to the very poor, let them run down and then abandoned them. Three high-rise towers of public housing, built only twenty years before had added to the decline of the neighborhood. By the time the city fathers of Springfield decided that the area was becoming a breeding ground for crime, disease and urban decay, these huge apartment houses were so dilapidated and had been vandalized so frequently by their frustrated tenants that the city was abandoning them.

At the time the redevelopment program was conceived, what city planners did to neighborhoods like the one in Springfield was to bring in large bulldozers, level everything in sight and start rebuilding an instant city from scratch.

But architect Switzer detested bulldozed landscapes. He also hated the word, "housing," much preferring "homes" or at least "apartments." He thought that small neighborhood shops might be preferable to large shopping centers in what formerly had been established neighborhoods. He also preferred tree-lined streets, front and back yards, and houses that did not look as if they had been built day before yesterday.

So, instead of calling in the bulldozers, he proposed that the city consider preserving what was there and what still might be saved. "There are many one, two and three family houses on those streets," he said in his report. "Save all you can. Keep the street patterns, including all the fine old trees that still stand. Preserve those backyards and front porches. Tear down only the houses that are now structurally unsound, and build so-called in-fill units (one or two family town houses of a style in keeping with the existing neighborhood) in the lots that become vacant when the unsafe houses are removed. Keep the neighborhood stores: they give life to the community. Add to the facilities that are already there as needed, but don't destroy anything when you don't have to."

"Most of all, give the families who will live in the new and refurbished homes a chance to own them, so that they can feel a sense of security and pride."

He suggested that no high-rise towers be built for families with children. But he recommended two special ten-story structures, one for old people who found that keeping up their own homes had become too burdensome, and another for young singles and couples with no children who did not want to be bothered with sweeping snow off stoops, tending gardens, and who, most of all, did not have to watch small children in the street from some remote apartment high above the ground. He pointed out that some other cities—Philadelphia, Boston and New Haven, for instance—had experimented with rebuilding neighborhoods in this way and that the experiments looked much more promising than the "housing" put up on the naked, bulldozed landscape.

It was not easy to find a private developer for such a plan, since it was obvious that no one, not the architect, nor the contractor, and not the sponsoring banks would make very much money out of such a project. It meant a lot of work with the members of the community, meetings to be attended, residents to be consulted, new families to be found to move into the area. But eventually, his plan was accepted. It was built and it worked. Children again play along the tree-lined streets in safety. There are several reasonably prosperous small Mom and Pop stores. Kids play ball on a few lots deliberately left empty, instead of strewing them with garbage. The crime rate is low, the quality of home maintenance is high. Occupancy is steady. There is an active and vocal neighborhood association.

At the time that Gilbert Switzer died, he was still trying to persuade the city of Springfield to improve the area. A wide highway-like road that seemed to lead to nowhere in particular separated the neighborhood from the waterfront of the Connecticut River, which borders the community. "Close that street, cover it with top soil, plant trees and shrubs so that the people in the community can use that river front for recreation, for jogging, for picnics, for fishing," he advised.

"A city is a city only if it's a series of communities," Gilbert Switzer used to say. "People have to care about themselves, their homes, their streets and their neighbors, or neighborhoods will decay and die." These days the bulldozed landscapes have gone out of fashion. There are several refurbished, lively city-scapes like the one in Springfield in other areas of the United States. Caring about the community is becoming increasingly important to planners and architects. And, perhaps, one of these days, that non-instant new town in Springfield will get its waterfront park.

17

The Cosmopolitan City: Istanbul

Cosmopolitan: 1) familiar with all the world; at home anywhere. 2) peopled from all the world, as a city.

The New American Webster's Dictionary

Of all structures, a bridge is the most civilizing and the most perilous. It may carry merchandise, armies, knowledge . . . a million humble and momentous exchanges . . . but it appears to stand only by the grace of chance and time. For some two thousand years, the metropolis of Istanbul, astride a narrow neck of water that divides Europe and Asia, has been such a bridge . . .

Colin Thobrun, "Istanbul"

The idea of a city as a bridge between two different cultures and life styles is picturesque and charming. But a city just isn't a bridge—the structure of an urban center is infinitely more complicated than that of a span between bodies of water. Istanbul is more cosmopolitan than any other city in the Middle East. A cosmopolitan city is one that contains elements of many cultures, ethnic groups and life styles. It can survive even if some of these elements clash, which in Istanbul they frequently do.

On the surface, Istanbul indeed has some bridgelike qualities: on nearby beaches and around hotel swimming pools, young Turkish women wear some of the briefest bikinis in the world, while in the bazaars and the older parts of the city their still-veiled sisters walk with jugs on their heads. On one corner a donkey cart or even an occasional camel may be blocking traffic . . . on another corner it's the latest model Mercedes or streetcar. There are streets in Istanbul that look like the downtown of a medium-sized slightly dilapidated American city (Newark, New Jersey, or Gary, Indiana, come to mind). But the view from a hill overlooking the Bosporus or the Sea of Marmara is one of surpassing loveliness and high romance, with the minarets of great mosques and the domes of ancient palaces silhouetted against a blue-gray sky. There are neon signs and oil lamps, modern air-conditioned apartment houses and ancient, ornate wooden houses with no plumbing or electricity, modern hospitals and old women who, for a few Turkish lira, will sell a sick person a green liquid or a charm to ward off "the evil eye."

Greeks, Russians, Armenians, Jews, Blacks, and Syrians live in Istanbul in an infinite number of ethnic quarters. The Turks have, over the centuries, welcomed refugees that could bring new skills or money to their country, but have occasionally also driven the newcomers out (or even massacred thousands of them) when they no longer served the national purpose.

At no time were the foreigners or their children truly absorbed into Turkish life. In that way, Istanbul is very different from New York, which many regard as the ultimate cosmopolitan city. New York also welcomed newcomers from other lands selectively, but once they had arrived, they were allowed to become part of the fabric of the city. Today in New York, there is still a Little Italy and a Chinatown. There is Yorkville, which is ethnically German, and parts of the Bronx that are ethnically Jewish. But the segregation is more economic than ethnic. Anyone with enough money to move can do so—and the old ethnic neighborhoods are often of most interest to tourists or nostalgia collectors.

This has not been true in Istanbul. Foreigners, even when they were welcomed and allowed to live in peace, have rarely become part of the fabric of the city. Unless they became very wealthy (in which case, they often moved to the United States or Canada), ethnic Greeks, Armenians, Jews, Russians and Blacks maintained their own neighborhoods, which many of them regarded as ghettos. Even today, they rarely mix with other Turks, almost never intermarry, and maintain their own foods, music, religion and culture. It is also very difficult for members of these minorities to rise from poverty. Most of Istanbul's ethnic ghettos are desperately poor, and the unemployment rate, high all over Turkey, is even higher among Greeks and Armenians than among ethnic Turks.

Greeks form the largest single minority in Turkey and in Istanbul. Greek families have been there for almost two thousand years, yet their descendants regard themselves as Greeks, not Turks. The Turks agree with this assessment.

The Greeks were welcomed when they came because they brought skills in seafaring and trading. Four-hundred years ago, one Turkish sultan was so worried that his Greek subjects might find more profitable pastures elsewhere, he guaranteed them protection not only for their lives and property, but also for their religion. Less than fifty years later, that promise was conveniently forgotten. For the Greeks, Istanbul has become the center of the Eastern Orthodox faith, and the Primate of Istanbul is the most important figure in that religion. But the church over which he presides is a shabby, dilapidated structure with none of the splendor and power of the Vatican. The government of Istanbul tolerates his presence in the city but gives no help or encouragement.

Over the centuries also, Greece and Turkey have been rivals. There have been territorial disputes. And during the times when the governments of the two countries have engaged in their regular disputes, the Greeks living in Turkey have been targets of discrimination and, occasionally, of violence. In recent years there have been anti-Greek riots with looting and firebombing whenever the dispute between Turkey and Greece over the island of Cyprus has heated up. No one seems to see the difference between Greeks living in Greece and Greeks whose families have been living in the Greek quarter of Istanbul for ten genera- tions.

The Armenians have fared even worse. In the eleventh century, they flourished, providing needed engineering, ar- chitectural and military skills. But, after a weak separatist movement was wiped out by the Turkish Army, Armenians became the most despised minority in Turkey. Between 1894 and 1896, 7,000 Armenian men, women and children were massacred in Istanbul. They fared worse in eastern provinces where, in 1915, more than a million ethnic Ar- menians were murdered. Following that orgy of killing, a million more sought to leave Turkey but found that they were not welcome anywhere in the world. Unlike the ethnic Greeks, they had no national homeland. However, the most gifted and most educated did leave—usually for the United States.

Today, there are still about 45,000 ethnic Armenians in Istanbul. Except for a few who through education have risen into the professional class, they live in a poverty- stricken section of the city, with high unemployment, a high infant mortality rate, and all the other sad statistics that afflict a ghetto. The few who have become wealthy through the professions, industry or commerce, or who have risen to influential posts in the university, tend to look upon their situations as temporary—there might be another anti- Armenian outbreak any year. Their sons and daughters talk of emigration to Europe, the United States or Canada.

Jews have found a haven in Turkey since the days of the Spanish Inquisition. At that time a colony of Spanish Jews settled in the section of Istanbul known as Balat. By the middle of the sixteenth century, one out of every ten citizens of Istanbul was of Jewish descent, more than forty thousand men, women and children. They became mer- chants, bankers, physicians and university professors and apparently felt that they had been totally integrated into the Turkish community. Then, in about 1665, a rabbi from

Smyrna, Sabbathai Levi, proclaimed himself Messiah and
urged Jews all over the Ottoman Empire (which included
all Turkey) to overthrow the Islamic regime of the Sultans.
He got as far as Istanbul, where the local government
caught up with him and threw him in prison. He was offered
a choice between being executed in a public square or con-
verting to Islam. He chose Islam and persuaded many of
his followers to join him in his new religion. Some of the
descendants of these Jews still live in Istanbul in a separate
quarter. They are called "donme." Their religion is officially
Islamic, but they are culturally and ethnically Jews.

With the defeat of Rabbi Levy, the ascendance of the
Jews in Istanbul slowly came to an end.

A new wave of Jewish immigrants arrived during the
late 1930s from Nazi Germany. Kemal Ataturk, the Turkish dictator, who in one generation tried to turn Turkey
from a backward Middle Eastern nation into a prosperous
and progressive Western one, admired Hitler and Mussolini
more than he did Churchill and Roosevelt. But he understood that Turkey needed the skills of these highly qualified
German Jews to grow in the direction he wishes his country
to go. So the entire educational system in Turkey is based
on the German model; the hospitals are staffed by doctors
trained in the skills the German Jewish professors brought
with them; and the Turkish textile industry uses German
methods of weaving and dying cloth. There are some
quarters of Istanbul in which German is almost a second
language. But many of these refugees from the Nazis and
their sons and daughters eventually migrated to Israel, leaving behind a pool of Turkish experts whom they had trained,
and who are now training a new generation of young ethnic
Turks.

Aristocratic and wealthy Russians descended on Istanbul in large numbers when the Communist revolution in
their own country turned them into refugees. In the antique
shops of Turkish cities and in the bazaar of Istanbul one
can find the lovely icons (pictures of saints), samovars
(which heated water for tea) and jewelry, which some of

these formerly rich Russians brought with them and sold in order to be able to survive. There are Russian restaurants, shops and churches in Istanbul today, but many of the refugees did not stay very long—they left for Paris, London and New York as soon as possible. If they could not make it out of Turkey, their sons and daughters often did.

Blacks arrived in Turkey as slaves. Their descendants stayed on, often as cooks in wealthy households. Some of the best restaurants in Istanbul are managed by descendants of these slaves. They too live in their own ghettos, rarely integrating into the Turkish fabric of the city.

But in spite of the tendency to keep their foreign settlers isolated, Istanbul has absorbed much of the special qualities that these newcomers brought with them. The cosmopolitan quality is evident everywhere in the life of the city: the many languages that are spoken, the kinds of food that are available, the type of education that is provided for Turkish children, even the kind of art, music and drama that is part of Istanbul's cultural scene.

In a deeper way, Turkey in general, and Istanbul in particular, have absorbed much of Western life: some good qualities and some very bad ones. Over the past fifty years or so, the government of Turkey has been more democratic than that of most of its Middle Eastern neighbors. More concern has been shown for education, health and welfare. There have been free clinics in Istanbul for decades, for instance. The literacy rate is higher than among most of Turkey's neighbors. There is a thriving, educated middle class. Taxes are high so that a small minority of super-wealthy do not dominate the country or the city the way they do in many of the oil-rich countries of the Middle East. It is possible for a gifted and lucky youngster, even one born into an ethnic minority, to rise from poverty through education.

The most striking difference between Turkey and its other Middle Eastern Islamic neighbors is the position of women. Kemal Ataturk, seeing the veil as the symbol of female oppression, outlawed it. Today there are still women in the Turkish countryside who hide their faces on the approach of a stranger, and some of these women eventually make their way to Istanbul. But overall, the women of the city enjoy a kind of freedom that they don't have anywhere else in the Middle East.

Universities are all coeducational, and entrance is by examination. Sex is not even considered. The same is true for government jobs. And since, in Turkey, most of the best jobs involve working for the government (in engineering and city planning offices, hospitals, clinics and universities), there is a surprisingly large number of gifted women in high posts. They help to run the social welfare system, are often in charge of designing and redesigning whole areas of cities, and are involved in planning highways, new schools and hospitals. The still-veiled women of Syria, Saudi Arabia and Jordan look upon their liberated Turkish sisters with awe and frequently with envy.

Ataturk also eliminated much of the power of the Islamic religion over other areas of secular life. Only civil marriages are allowed in Turkey. The fez (a sign of class as well as religion) was outlawed, right along with the veil. Today the only fezes available in Istanbul are sold to American, German and Japanese tourists in the bazaar. While the vast majority of Turks belong to the Islamic faith, the civil law in Turkey is based on the Napoleonic code of France and British Common law, not the Koran. Although Istanbul's skyline is dominated by the minarets of hundreds of mosques, and although the chant of the Islamic crier calling the faithful to prayer is heard regularly in Istanbul's streets, much of the city's way of life is cosmopolitan, not Islamic.

Of course, along with many of the advantages the West had to offer Istanbul, some of the disadvantages are also evident. Istanbul, for instance, has tried to impose modern traffic patterns, complete with thousands of automobiles, on its ancient streets and alleys. As a result, the worst traffic jams in the world occur in Istanbul. There are days when some drivers simply leave their cars stuck in traffic and walk home, hoping to come back for the cars after the rush hour (which seems to go on and on) ends. Buses get stuck, too, and hundreds of cursing, sweating commuters may spend hours either waiting for a bus to get moving again or walking wherever they are going, home or to work. Government offices and stores often open late because the employees just could not make it to work through the dense traffic.

The situation is sometimes made worse by the sporadic way in which government-operated utilities run. Electricity throughout the city may suddenly be cut off—and right along with it all traffic lights. This tends to make a ride in an automobile even more hazardous than it is even under normal conditions. In recent years, the city of Istanbul has instituted a system of driver's licenses, but apparently many Turks still drive without a knowledge of traffic rules. Most of the cars, buses and trucks are very old. It is not unusual to see a large truck parked on a hillside with stones holding the tires in place. The brakes gave up working years ago. As a result, Turkey in general, and Istanbul in particular, has one of the highest motor vehicle accident rates in the world.

Since electricity and other forms of power were regarded as necessities for the modernization program envisioned by Ataturk, electrical plants were built quickly. Turkey, unlike its Arab neighbors, has very little oil; most of the electricity, along with much industrial production, is powered by soft coal. A cloud of pollution often hangs over Istanbul, obscuring the magical beauty of the view over the Golden Horn. Since everyone agrees that without the power generated by coal almost all the activity of the country would come to a dead stop, no environmentalists protest air pollution.

Ataturk's reforms brought roads, schools, hospitals and electric plants to much of Turkey. They also brought to millions of villagers the knowledge that a different kind of life existed elsewhere. Before Ataturk, there were villagers living within fifty miles of Istanbul who did not know the city existed. They had never been further from home than a donkey loaded down with enough water for the return trip could carry them. The life of the village, no matter how poor, was all they had ever known.

Now, with modern roads carrying hundreds of ancient buses through the countryside, the villagers have a chance to see what life beyond a fifty-mile radius of their homes can be. At first only the men migrated to the cities, leaving women and children behind to continue working the dried-up, exhausted land. The men would return once or twice a year for a brief visit but would live, usually three or four to a cellar or tenement, in the cities where they did the kind of menial work that even the poverty-stricken city dwellers did not want. Today wives and children insist on joining the men in the cities. Some experts in rural life blame the transister radio for this development. Television is, of course, not available to Turkish villagers, but the men bring home the little radios as presents . . . and the women and children hear about places like Istanbul, which seem magical to them.

So, in an increasing flood, whole families arrive in Istanbul from villages to find jobs that don't exist, to look for housing they can't afford and to overcrowd hospitals and social services. Outside of every Turkish city, including Istanbul, are the "gichicondas"—the instant slums made up of old wooden crates, tin cans, corrugated steel stolen from a construction site. There live the villagers, who at first consider their miserable home as a temporary place. Later they find that it is permanent—there is no other place to go. Of course, the gichicondas have no electricity, no sewers, and the only water often comes from a community well. Still the villagers stay, there is a hope for them in the city that is lacking in the village. They have seen how richer people live, and they want a share of that good life, as do millions of other country people who crowd into the cities all over the world.

These villagers present the city government of Istanbul with an enormous problem. They are ethnic Turks, who cannot be encouraged, through neglect or terror, to move on. They are in the cities to stay, and the government has to take some responsibility for them. Turkey is a poor country, and Istanbul shares that poverty. There is no oil to export, no agricultural surplus, no manufactured goods. Turkey's best hope for much-needed money—American dollars, German marks and Japanese yen that can be used to build houses and provide the services these new city dwellers need—is the tourist. And yet, the influx of the poor may affect the growing tourist industry in Turkey. The average person on a holiday does not want to see misery. The Turkish Office of Tourism knows this and tries to keep the gichiconda dwellers from coming to the bazaars, museums, mosques and hotels that the tourists frequent. There have been occasional fights between the poor and the police.

Turkey has had a fairly stable government since Ataturk assumed power years ago. But within the past decade, there have been episodes of unrest in Istanbul and other large cities. University students have often joined the poverty-stricken gichiconda families to protest conditions. And occasionally there have been acts of terrorism against members of the government and foreigners, who are considered to be responsible for Turkey's poverty. Meanwhile, more Turks arrive in Istanbul from the country every day.

So Istanbul, like other cities, faces problems that will have to be solved eventually. In many ways, because of its cosmopolitan nature and its long experience with newcomers to the city, Istanbul is in a better position to deal with at least some of the worst difficulties. As a city, because of its location and its history, it will undoubtedly survive. But to maintain what is beautiful and to deal with what is terrible in the city, everything that the city fathers can learn from the past will have to be used. And that may mean, first of all, accepting all those ethnic Greeks and Jews and Armenians and Russians as Turks and citizens of Istanbul, and using their combined experience in a joint endeavor to face the difficulties ahead.

18

Venice: The Museum City

Venice is the most beautiful city in the world. Yet in describing it, I have difficulty. I fear you will be bored. Many people do get bored in Venice, precisely because it is so beautiful. They do not like to say so, because a visit to Venice costs a great deal of money. But Venetians know all about it, and don't want a visitor to stay too long anyway. It could have been a Venetian who coined the telling phrase: "Guests are like fish. After three days they stink."

Aubrey Menen, *Venice*

Venice, like all other great cities in the world, was founded for a very practical reason: in this case, fear. The founders were a group of men and women who lived at a time when the Roman Empire was declining in power. In the fifth century, Attila the Hun came over the Alps, and the Roman army was too disorganized and too weak to stop him. He used some effective and old-fashioned methods to win his wars: he massacred all who tried to stop him and burned down every building in sight. The idea was to keep resistance at a minimum by demoralizing the enemy, who often fled before Attila's army even appeared on the scene.

Among the first to take the hint were a group of merchants and sailors who lived in a Roman territory we now call Veneto. They were accustomed to the sea, and Attila and his troops were not. So they decided that the safest place for them would be a group of islands off their coastline. They founded Venice in about 450 A.D. And their idea proved to be a good one. Attila and other conquerors decided not to bother them.

But space on the islands was limited, and more and more Romans began moving into the new town. So the Venetians decided to colonize the waters around the islands. They adopted a method of building that had been used since prehistoric times in some areas of northern Italy. They built their houses, palaces and churches on piles sunk deeply into the hard mud that surrounded the islands. Then they deepened the waterways between their rows of buildings to form canals in which their boats could move easily. It turned out that, even after Attila and his murderous hordes had disappeared from the area, this building plan proved to be practical and economical. The city continued to expand. Because of its location and its easy accessibility by water, Venice eventually became one of the merchant capitals of the world.

At first the city was run in what for the times was a remarkably democratic manner, with an elected council. But the people soon found that democracy, even though it seemed to be the fairest form of government, was not efficient enough to suit their purposes. So they decided that one-man rule would suit them better. That man was chosen by the most powerful merchant families in Venice and was called "Il Duce" (the leader). A twentieth century dictator, Benito Mussolini, chose the same title about nine hundred years later. But in Venice, to conform with local dialect, "Il Duce" became "Il Doge." That's how the group of rulers known as the "doges," who ran Venice for about two hundred years got their name.

On the surface, the doges were all-powerful. But actually the city was run by a group of exceedingly wealthy merchant families whose names were inscribed in what the Venetians called "The Golden Book." Known to the world as "The Worthies," these merchants had become the middlemen for much of the trade between the East and the West; whether the items traded were silks, spices or slaves, the Worthies received a cut of the profits.

They also managed to develop one of the most advanced shipbuilding businesses in the world and became the finest navigators since the Phoenicians. As Aubrey Menen puts it: "The Phoenicians built Carthage on the profits of trade. Carthage has gone, and not a stone of it remains above ground. The Venetians built Venice, and it is still the glory and marvel of Western civilization. We owe the alphabet to the Phoenicians because they needed it for record-keeping. We owe Venice to very similar businessmen who built it to show off."

Like many businesses today, they had excellent advice when it came to art and architecture. They hired only the best, often early in these gifted men's careers, when, apparently, they were still affordable. Nowhere in the world is there such an abundance of the works of the men who, in the next decade or so, would become the finest and busiest artists of their age. And, as businessmen with a great deal of money and power will often do, the Venetian merchants took chances. They allowed the artists they employed to be innovative, to develop their own style. St. Mark's Cathedral has traces of Syria and Constantinople, but it is built in a highly original architectural form. The Palace of the Doges, which the merchants commissioned to be the most wildly luxurious building in the world, is still regarded as just that by most art historians. There is such a profusion of painting, mosaic work, gilt carvings and jeweled artifacts that it confuses the first-time visitor and then impresses him like no other palace in Europe. That's, of course, exactly what the Worthies had in mind when they appropriated the money to construct it. And as the doges lost power to the businessmen who really ran the city, the furnishings and works of art in the building became more extravagant. The ruling merchants were shrewd enough to want to keep their alleged leader happy. If he didn't have real power, he should have the ultimate in luxury and ceremonial courtesy so that he would not turn against them.

As it turned out, the Worthies had much better advice in the arts than they did in the area that should have logically concerned them most: business. Looking back on Venetian history, one comes to the inevitable conclusion that Venice was unintentionally built to become what it now is: a museum city, with no other purpose than to attract lovers of beauty in art. It is evident now that as trade routes to the East changed, the world could bypass Venice. When middlemen were no longer needed, other cities in Europe became commercial centers.

What finally sealed Venice's doom as a commercial port, though, was the ability of the Portuguese to build even better ships and develop new and revolutionary methods of navigation. By the time the sixteenth century began, Venice already was looked upon by the rich and powerful of Europe as a center of recreation and artistic excellence rather than as a practical place in which to conduct the business of commerce and industry. A whole suburb, the Brenta, attracted the newly rich from what is now Italy and France. Glorious palaces were built on the outskirts, many designed by Andrea Palladio (1508–1580), one of the most outstanding architects of his age. The villas he built were grand, but practical, as many of the Venetian palaces were not. He invented systems of disposing of sewage and obtaining clean water. The traffic to and from the Brenta was carefully calculated and controlled. Like today's suburbanites, the European upper classes didn't like to be caught in traffic jams, though they used canals instead of roads. The boatways were made wide enough and deep enough to allow easy passage from the center of Venice to the luxurious homes in the Brenta. Life moved outward from the center of the city. Looking at Venice today, one can see how the pattern of life changed as Venice became a center for culture and the good life, but no longer one for commerce. Had the city been less beautiful, it probably would have died, as did many other urban centers that lost their usefulness.

In the long run, it was the sense of art and artistry that the Worthies displayed when they built their city that helped it to survive, rather than the power and the glory of its early days. Even the geography, which at first made it a safe haven from invading armies, and later a logical stop for Eastern trade, started to work against it. By the middle of the eighteenth century, Venice had begun to sink. Again, had the city been less beautiful, it might well have been abandoned. But now the world at large had developed an interest in Venice; and as the buildings crumbled or shifted, they were quickly restored.

By the nineteenth century, Venice had become the capital of romantic dreams. Poets from all over the earth came there and wrote about its incredible beauty and fascination. Along with the beauty, there was an air of decay and decadence about the city that often fascinated the poets even more than its pure loveliness. In today's literature, art and films, Venice is often used as a symbol of sinister seduction: beauty with a hidden core of evil.

What about the real Venice today, not the tourist city or the literary image? After all, Venetians live there and have to deal with its day-to-day problems. Perhaps the men who most combine Venice's romantic allure with its practical difficulties are the gondoliers; to listen to a gondolier talk about the city he loves but finds maddeningly difficult to cope with can be very interesting.

Georgio is such a gondolier. He is a sharp businessman who supports a wife and six children with his decorative boat. He knows what's expected of him: jokes, compliments for women tourists (especially middle-aged ones) and occasionally, a song. He knows that "Santa Lucia" isn't Venetian at all—it's Neapolitan; and like many residents of northern Italy, Georgio considers Naples distinctly inferior to his town. But he knows that the tourists like that song. He can also sing "Three Coins in the Fountain," knowing it comes from an American movie he has never seen, and is about Rome, not Venice. He learned the words from a recording, by sound, he says. He hasn't a clue what they mean and doesn't consider such knowledge necessary. "I'm not an artist, I'm a businessman," he says, unconsciously echoing the Worthies of another age. But that is about all that Georgio has in common with the rich and powerful of the old days.

Because, behind the golden palaces and shining white marble churches that front the main canals, Venice today is a gigantic, stinking slum.

Georgio and his family live in a house on a small canal that has become the sewer, as well as the street. The house has no workable indoor plumbing, no central heating, no adequate supply of clean, running water. Its once handsome stucco exterior is cracking and peeling. During spring and fall rainstorms, water floods the first floor. Georgio's wife has learned to pile all the furniture on top of the sofa as soon as she sees storm clouds gathering, to keep her tables and chairs from swimming out her front door. There are rats as large as cats and mosquitos that look as if they came out of some science fiction movie. But worst of all, there are no jobs for the children once they reach adolescence, except as porters and kitchen helpers in the many hotels and pensiones that are the principle industry of Venice.

"My children are leaving one by one. They don't come back except for holidays. I can't blame them. There really is nothing for them here," Georgio says sadly. Usually he doesn't admit that anything is wrong with his beloved Venice; but on an evening when yet another flood was threatening, and he had to tie his gondola to one of the many docks, he was depressed. On a bad night with rain about to pour into his living room for the third time in a month, surrounded by tourists whom he does not especially like or respect, but needs to maintain his livelihood, he grumbles and talks of departing to a better climate. Georgio has to admit to himself that, from the point of view of a

Venetian today, who lives in a house instead of a palace, Venice leaves a good deal to be desired.

He would like to drive a car, he says. He'd rather have a machine do the work of transportation rather than his body. But, of course, there are no cars in Venice . . . only boats of all kinds. And some of those boats bother him too. "Venice has got to be the noisiest place on the face of the earth," he says. "The racket of those motor launches we use as streetcars, the barges that bring in all our food, the small racing boats that some of the young rich boys run through the canals day and night . . . enough is enough." He doesn't believe that New York's Lexington Avenue on a Saturday night can actually be even noisier.

Also, he would like electric lights that can be counted upon to work in cold and wet weather. "Lanterns and oil lamps are romantic, at least that's what the tourists tell me," he says. "But you can't really see when the electricity is off, and I have to stay in the gondola to make sure that it's not drifting off with the tide and the winds. Have you ever sat in a gondola on a wet, cold night? I wouldn't recommend it as an evening's entertainment. You may think that gondoliers sing a lot. We curse more than we sing."

Giorgio's wife, besides wishing that she could see her grown-up children and her one grandchild more often, wishes that they could have a washing machine, electric stove and other appliances she sees on her television. She would like plumbing that works, floors that do not need scrubbing after every rain storm and the knowledge that her youngest is safe playing on the sidewalk without being in constant danger of falling into the canal or being bitten by a rat.

And then there is the smell, especially on a hot, damp evening. The back canals of Venice are strewn with litter and garbage. The flood tides that were supposed to clean the canals have long since been reduced to ineffectiveness because the main canals and the lagoon on which Venice is located had to be excavated to make room for larger ships. So the garbage stays, putrifies and stinks. There are the motorized garbage collection gondolas, of course, but they concentrate on the main canals, and frequently, all the garbage men go on strike.

Overshadowing all these complaints is the fear that because of the lowering water table, Venice is actually sinking into the sea. "We dropped one centimeter over the past ten years," Georgio's wife says. "And they tell us that the beautiful buildings on the Piazza San Marco that the tourists come to see are falling apart because of the fumes that reach Venice from the oil refineries across the water. If the tourists don't come here any more, what will become of all of us?" Georgio's wife may not admire or respect tourists very much, but like Georgio she knows that their livelihood depends on these hordes of Germans, Japanese and American men, women and children who descend on Venice as soon as the cold, damp winds and floods of winter have passed, and who sit in the sidewalk cafes that border the Piazza San Marco, looking out over the Cathedral and the Doges' Palace. They buy souvenirs of the city, which one of her sons sells; and for some strange reason that Georgio's wife fails to understand, they like to have their pictures taken with pigeons sitting on the most exposed parts of their bodies. Georgio's wife hates pigeons a lot more than she dislikes tourists. To her, "those filthy, miserable birds" are just one more of the nuisances of Venetian life.

Georgio's wife may not know it, but over the centuries, tourists, who loved the beauty of Venice without having to cope with its day-to-day problems, have repeatedly raised the money that has kept Venice alive, even as a museum.

Without the help of engineers who used every method they could devise to stabilize the water table and to keep the floods at bay, Venice would probably have sunk into the sea long ago. Without experts in chemistry and architecture, most of the city's great buildings would have been corroded by acrid smoke from the oil refineries across the lagoon in the industrial centers of Maghera and Mestre, two towns that are, technically, suburbs of Venice.

Recently the city fathers of Venice have tried to get a law passed allowing them to secede from their suburbs, probably the only instance of an inner city wishing to rid itself of its suburban areas. The city fathers, most of whom live along the most beautiful of the Venetian canals, realized suddenly that they could not sue their own suburbs for the pollution that was destroying their city. It was not this, however, but the pressure of the international art community that finally persuaded some of the twentieth century "Worthies" in the industrial suburbs to attempt some kind of pollution control. As a result, the destruction by chemical pollution of Venetian art treasures has been slowed considerably, because the industrial plants across the lagoon have begun to spew forth less smoke. And for reasons that no one fully understands, Venice has not only stopped sinking, it's even rising a little.

At first nobody in Venice would believe that the city was not about to be destroyed by flood. After all, generations of Venetians have been brought up with the notion that eventually the water would rise over the top of the dome of St. Mark's Cathedral. But Dr. Paolo Gatto, a senior geologist in the state-run National Research Council, insisted that, after years of observation and laboratory study, the conclusion was inescapable: Venice was rising again, slowly. The measurements taken over the last seven years by Dr. Gatto's organization, called the Laboratory for the Study of Large Masses, showed that the water pressure under Venice was building up, allowing the city to stabilize.

Dr. Gatto suspects that one of the reasons the water table is more stable is that the excessive pumping of water from artesian wells by industry in Maghera has all but ceased. With water available from other sources, many of the industries have capped those wells and are no longer pumping the water out. This allows the water level below Venice to remain stable, and even to rise a little. But the floods will continue for a long time to come. If Venice continues in its present course, it may rise about two centimeters in the next century, another researcher, Professor Alberto A. Tomasin of the University of Venice, announced recently. Since waters up to half a meter have been known to flood St. Mark's Square, that does not seem like much improvement, but it should reassure Georgio's wife. At least her grandmother's worst predictions about the eventual fate of Venice: "One day it will sink without a trace. Only those with boats will be rescued. It's a good thing that Papa has a gondola, that's even better than Noah's ark," will probably not come true.

Also, according to some recent studies, the general exodus from Venice seems to have slowed. For the past five years the census has shown a stable population of 100,000 as well as a stable water table. The chances are that Venice will be there to be admired by our children and grandchildren—and that, perhaps, the youngest of Georgio's children will stay, instead of moving on to the industrial plants across the lagoon.

Are there other museum cities in the world? None as beautiful as Venice, but there are indeed other cities that the industrial age has passed by and that are surviving because tourists find them lovely enough to visit and support. Saltzburg in Austria and Katmandu in Nepal might be looked upon as museum cities, for instance. Cartagena, Columbia, survives partly on its beauty and partly because it has become a center for illegal drug trade. Agra, India, receives much of its income from visitors to the legendary Taj Mahal, the most elaborate tomb ever erected to commemorate the death of one woman by her husband. It is said that the men who put together the lovely building made of sandstone and white marble, embellished with thousands of semipricious stones, had their hands chopped off when they had finished the construction just to make sure that no similar building would ever be erected anywhere else in the world.

Are we still building museum cities? Probably not, because we can't afford them. Instead, we tend to section off parts of our cities as "cultural centers," on which we construct buildings that can help the city "show off" just as the Worthies did in Venice. Sometimes the centers actually add a great deal to the life of the city. Lincoln Center in New York may not be the architectural equivalent of the Piazza San Marco in Venice or the Taj Mahal in Agra, but it did rescue a New York slum area from complete decay.

Instead of building monuments to the good taste of our city fathers, we build monuments to commerce and industry. One of the most impressive and expensive buildings in an urban renewal area of New Haven, Connecticut, is a huge parking garage designed in poured, reinforced concrete by architect Paul Rudolph. It looks quite a lot like the Roman Coliseum.

In other cities, pre-existing beauty has been given a business reason for continuing to exist. Kyoto, Japan was once the imperial capital of that nation. It has some of the most beautiful gardens, temples and palaces on earth. But the Japanese are realists: they reasoned that few tourists would come from Europe and America just to view their historical and botanic splendors. On the other hand, destroying all that beauty offended their sensibilities. So they simply added a commercial and industrial section to the already existing beauty. Today, businessmen from all over the world love to go to Kyoto to transact their million dollar or yen or Deutsche mark or Swiss franc deals. After the meetings they can sit in one of the temple gardens and imagine themselves back in the Imperial Japan of centuries ago. Kyoto is an international trade center precisely because it is also a museum city.

According to art historians, we probably stopped building museum cities with the Industrial Revolution. At this point, we have to make sure that we keep the ones built by our ancestors so that our children and grandchildren can visit and enjoy them. Different cities have found different solutions to maintain their historical and artistic assets: Venice has counted on its architectural and artistic beauty to keep itself alive; Salzburg created the Mozart Festival; Kyoto added a whole new business section to its historical district. There are as many solutions to survival as there are cities. But every time a beautiful city dies, the world is that much poorer.

19

Commercial Cities:
Amsterdam and
Hong Kong

Kung Hei Fat Choy (Rejoice and grow rich)

A favorite Hong Kong toast

In many ways, Amsterdam has a great deal in common with
Venice. It lies several feet below sea level and is, therefore,
also in constant danger of floods. But Amsterdam, unlike
Venice, has always been protected from the waters by a
carefully designed and maintained system of dikes and
dams. No one even remembers a time when water has
flooded the living rooms of residents along the great canals
of Amsterdam, as it does the living rooms of those who
live along the canals in Venice.

Amsterdam was first settled somewhat later than
Venice, but its principal growth occurred at about the same
time the Worthies of Venice began to build up their town.
Unlike Venice, which grew rather without a plan, the careful businessmen who built Amsterdam planned carefully.
From the tiny, medieval fishing village on the river Amstel,
Amsterdam (the name obviously comes from the river and
the dams that hold it and the ocean waters at bay) grew
until, in the seventeenth century, it was a major port and
commercial center for all of Europe.

The original semi-circular layout for the city included

Canal Cities

The sixteenth century city fathers who planned
Venice did not think of the future. That's why the city no
longer works, except as a gigantic museum. The lovely
façades and squares attract tourists, but the buildings that
front many of the side canals are crumbling slums.
Gondoliers who live in these houses would probably
exchange them gladly for a less romantic and more livable
home. Italian Government Travel Office

The sixteenth century city fathers who planned the
canal city of Amsterdam thought of the future. The city still
works as a commercial center for the world. Netherlands
National Tourist Office

three great concentric canals: the Herrengracht, the gentle-man's canal; the Prinsengracht, the Prince's canal; and the Keizersgracht, the Emperor's canal, all dug deep and wide enough for goods to be transported by barge and sailing ship to most parts of the city. Later, other canals and waterways were developed so that smaller ships could be anchored almost anywhere in the old Amsterdam.

Like the Venetians, the men who built Amsterdam were merchants. They planned the city carefully, but unlike the Venetians, they were not motivated by a desire for pomp and luxury. What they needed was more practical. "They wanted to provide housing for merchants, craftsmen and refugees, build a showplace that would reflect Amster-dam's commercial greatness, and most important of all, create conditions for trade by sea," says Hans Koning in his book, *Amsterdam*. The city fathers planned so well that their initial schemes still work today, in the latter part of the twentieth century, with very little obvious change. Am-sterdam today is still a commercial center of the Western world.

Those who planned the canal system had no model to work from. They knew about Venice, but considered that city's system, correctly as it turned out, to be quite inade-quate. They understood that they would need more rather than less waterways than Venice, even though they planned a system of streets to run along the canals, which Venice had not considered necessary. They built over the years 600 canals, more than twice the number built in Venice, on an area of about two thousand acres.

The waterways were dug entirely by men wielding picks and shovels. (According to Koning, the word "gracht" literally means "to dig" in English.) They made sure that a constant water level was maintained to eliminate the kind of flooding and sinking that is an integral part of Venice's problems and one of the reasons for its decline from a living, working city to a museum.

What's more, those who planned the Dutch city were

concerned with sanitation even in those very early days
when such problems as sewage and garbage were furthest
from the minds of other city planners. The dams or dikes
of Amsterdam were built to allow fresh water and, in some
cases, sea water to clean out debris and waste every twenty-
four hours. Amsterdamers are proud of the fact that the
water in their canals is almost pure enough to drink. Fish
and all sorts of other water animals live in these canals.
During the spring and summer, hundreds of Dutch families
sit along the sides of the main canals catching their evening
meal of eel and other popular fish. Drinking the water from
a Venice canal would most probably result in death from
typhoid, dysentery and other exotic diseases . . . and no
fish have lived in those canals for more than half a century.

The system devised in the early seventeenth century
was so effective that it worked until about 1876, when
those who ran the city noted that too much mud was silting
into the canals from the sea. In that year, the clever engineers of Amsterdam made their first mistake: they built
a dam across their harbor to prevent the mud from flowing
in. Because the dam checked not only the silting, but also
the flow of the tides into the canals, the water in the canals
quickly became stagnant. Contemporary accounts tell of
water turning bright red over night. Some citizens believed
that God was punishing the city for what they perceived as
evil ways. (Most other Europeans had always considered
the Dutch as models of private and public virtue.) Engineers
saw the problem almost at once: they had to devise a way
to stop the silting while still allowing the tides to cleanse
the canals. They built a system of sluices into the dam,
which allows sea water to flow into the canals on a regulated
basis while keeping the mud out. The system worked well
until 1932, when because of the growing population of the
city and the need for more water and electricity, the mouth
of the Amstel River (the Zuider Zee) was cut off from the
open sea by yet another dam constructed across its mouth.
Being practical, the Dutch raised the land behind the dam

and used it to grow agricultural products. The canals are now cleaned by fresh water pumped through them from the lake that was formerly the Zuider Zee.

Modern Amsterdam has 750,000 inhabitants, over seven times as many as Venice, and the city is still growing. A quarter of these people live in the suburbs, linked by an excellent road and rail system to the central part of the city, which is still one of the most important commercial centers in the world.

Unlike Venice, Amsterdam has a system of roads, as well as river transportation. Like most other major cities, it has its occasional traffic jams at morning and afternoon rush hours. But even in their approach to traffic, the residents of Amsterdam have shown their good sense. Almost everyone who is not too young, too old or crippled rides a bicycle to work, to school, and even to formal evening parties. It is not unusual to see a man in evening clothes bike up to the entrance of Amsterdam's main concert hall, or a flock of bikes parked in front of the city's most elegant nightclubs and restaurants. Every major business has its bike racks, as well as parking lots.

Holland is small and all its cities are densely populated, but one never gets the feeling of crowding. Trees line the streets and the banks of the canals. There are many open parks. Even in the center of the city there are houses with gardens behind them. And the canals themselves have been used as a kind of auxiliary housing site. Many of them are lined with houseboats, attached to permanent moorings, in which families live. Some of these houseboats are very luxurious and are among the most expensive living accommodations one can buy or rent in Amsterdam. To deal with any problems that might arise, there is also a houseboat that contains a police station; and to care for the many homeless cats that are one of Amsterdam's constant worries, there is a barge that contains a cat hospital and temporary shelter for them. It's supported by taxes, but many Amsterdamers leave legacies in their wills to the cat boat, so the animals live in almost as much luxury as the residents of the luxurious houseboats.

Amsterdam, unlike many of its competitors in the commercial world, seems to be remarkably free of urban nuisances and problems. It is pollution free, since Holland was one of the first countries in the world to apply strict emission control standards to its factories and even to its automobiles and trucks. It is clean, because littering is considered exceedingly bad form by the Dutch, who are just as avid in chasing dirt and debris as they are competent in turning goods and services into money. It is beautiful because, for centuries, nothing has been built that did not conform to an exacting and carefully thought out city plan.

Many of the beautiful houses that line the canals were built about the same time as those crumbling palaces in Venice. The difference is that Amsterdam houses were built to be useful and lived in . . . and they have continued to be lived in by generation after generation of Dutch families. When mechanical plumbing and electricity became part of standard urban life, the houses were adapted to these new elements, but they were never allowed to change in their outward appearance. Built on piles set in the mud just like the buildings in Venice, the Amsterdam houses were not allowed to crack, sink or peel. If anything, those elegant buildings in Old Amsterdam probably look better today, and are certainly more livable and useful, than they did when they were first constructed four hundred years ago.

Amsterdam has always dealt in goods and services that were deemed necessary by the world at large. Unlike Venice, the city fathers have been able to adapt to changing needs. When silks and spices of the East began to filter into Europe through ports other than Venice and Amsterdam, the Dutch simply began exporting goods that were unique to their own economy: agricultural products and preserved fish. They realized that their country was not suited to heavy industry, so they turned to producing two commodities that required little space and did not pollute the atmosphere of their cities: diamonds, cut and polished, and plant bulbs. Dutch diamonds and Dutch tulip bulbs are the best in the world.

In Amsterdam, they developed a system of banks and credit institutions that served the needs of other much larger cities and countries. Some of the world's most powerful bankers live and work in those picturesque seventeenth century houses along the canals, although there are now some high-rise office buildings in parts of Amsterdam where they will not compete with or destroy the image of that dignified, unified seventeenth century city.

The city fathers of Amsterdam, as they grew rich and powerful, shared the desire of the Worthies of Venice to show off their riches by commissioning architects and artists to provide the city with some of their best work. Again, they did not want expensive pomp that might not serve the city well in the future. There are few gigantic statues in Amsterdam. Instead there are small fountains. The paintings that grace the city's museums were obviously meant to be hung in the homes of the burghers who commissioned them. Rembrandt depended upon the generosity of the burghers who came to him to have portraits painted of themselves and of family members. One of his most famous paintings, *Night Watch,* is actually a group portrait of some of the richest and most powerful merchants in Amsterdam during Rembrandt's lifetime. Other painters also depended on subsidies from the city fathers to continue their work, much of which now hangs in Amsterdam's excellent museums.

In more recent times, a group of radical activists have made proposals for change and for improving city life, but in ways no other group of radicals in the world have chosen. The Provos (short for provocateur) first gained prominence during the time between the announcement of Princess Beatrice's engagement to a German prince, Claus van Amsberg, and their wedding. The Prince served in the German army during World War II and Holland was occupied by

German troops, so the marriage was highly unpopular with
a great many Dutch citizens, and the Provos (not to be
confused with the Northern Irish Provos, a violent branch
of the revolutionary and outlawed Irish Republican Army)
organized a variety of protests. From the beginning, their
tactics were different from similar groups everywhere. They
evoked embarrassment, irritation and bewilderment among
the Dutch establishment, but they also evoked a great deal
of laughter . . . and for that reason, they may have been
more effective than their dead serious, grimly determined
counterparts in other lands.

The demonstrators did throw an occasional smoke
bomb, but that was as far as their violence went. Usually,
they paraded with their faces painted as clowns, or dressed
up in outlandish costumes. When Amsterdam police over-
reacted to one such demonstration and tried to break up
the gathering with rubber nightsticks, the Provos armed
themselves with sticks of rhubarb.

Nor did the young demonstrators expect a great deal.
They were quite realistic (as Dutchman seem to be in most
phases of their public and private life) as to what could
be accomplished. "If only we could be revolutionaries,"
wrote one of their leaders, Roel Van Duyn, a student at
Amsterdam University. "We cannot convince the masses,
we scarcely even want to . . . we are more than likely to
see the sun rise in the west than a revolution in the Netherlands. We know our actions are useless: we are quite ready
to believe that neither President Johnson (then President
of the United States) nor Prime Minister Kosygin of the
USSR will listen to us, and for that reason, we are free to
do what we like."

Eventually, some of the friendly demonstrations did
turn into what in Holland is considered street violence. In
most other countries they would be considered a mild dis-
turbance of the peace. After a major encounter with the
Establishment, the Provos decided to enter politics. In 1966,
Provo candidates were nominated for posts on the Amster-

dam Municipal Council, and they actually polled enough votes (13,000) to obtain one seat for one of their representatives.

Many of the plans they proposed seem almost prophetic. They foresaw the gasoline shortage, the energy shortage, the pollution disasters and other kinds of ills that are now part of life in most cities.

Their political program was a set of "white plans"— i.e., white, electrically-powered cars would be bought by the city and made available to anyone who needed transportation on a "use it and leave it" basis for a small subscription fee. The city would acquire a fleet of white bikes to be used by anyone who preferred pedal power to electricity. Chimneys would be painted white as a symbol against air pollution and would have to be kept white, to make sure that the symbol became an actual fact. Housing earmarked for destruction would be painted white and made available, free-of-charge, to the homeless.

Much of what the Provos planned never happened. But the white cars actually were tried. Operated by batteries that needed to be recharged regularly, and having a top speed of twenty miles per hour, they were first put into service in 1974. Unfortunately they did not catch on. Amsterdamers called them "pickle jars on wheels" and continued to prefer automobiles, bikes and their feet as means of transportation. With the gasoline shortage getting worse worldwide, however, authorities are now taking a second look at these cars, and representatives of other city governments in Europe and in the United States have been in touch with the Dutch inventor of the cars to see if they might be adapted for urban use in other parts of the world.

There was one major goal that the Provos did reach, however, and that was a municipal subsidy for all artists working seriously in Amsterdam. In that, the city went right back to its Renaissance origin. The City Arts Council purchases on a regular basis the work of many sculptors, painters, potters, weavers and other artists and craftspeople. The scheme is called B.K.R., which in Dutch stands for Artists

Arrangement. Artists and artisans sell their work to the town in which they live, and it is exhibited in schools and public buildings. With true Dutch practicality, prices are fixed in such a way that the artist is able to live on the proceeds of one sale until he or she is ready for the next. The artists are expected to get enough money for their work to enjoy a modest but adequate standard of living—they get about as much for their work as they would get were they on the Dutch version of Social Security, which provides much more adequately for the needs of Dutch citizens than the Social Security system of the United States. What's more, artists who cannot afford to live on their sales often get a rent-free or rent-subsidized studio in which to live and work. Amsterdamers now, as in the Renaissance, believe that when commerce and industry combine with beauty and art, a city will live, thrive and improve.

Amsterdam has its problems, as do all cities. In recent years waves of new immigrants from former Dutch colonies (Indonesia was the largest) have settled in the city. The newcomers are strangers to much of what has made Dutch life so uniformly pleasant. They don't have the Dutch passion for cleanliness and order, for instance. Many citizens of Amsterdam, who have always prided themselves on their tolerance of strange customs and ideas, find themselves bothered by the noise, disorder and what they perceive as lack of discipline and cleanliness in the newcomers. They wonder if they can keep their city in the same pleasant, leisurely, orderly and prosperous state it was in when they inherited it from their parents and grandparents. As urban areas go, Amsterdam has to be one of the most attractive cities on the face of the earth, though its origins were in trade.

Hong Kong is still a different commercial city. Its origins are fairly recent. One hundred and fifty years ago, Hong Kong was a sleepy fishing port. But a British Navy captain, Charles Eliot, had the foresight to envision a major trade post and harbor there. He insisted that China cede the small town plus some twenty-nine square miles of surrounding rock and sand to the British. He got fired for his pains: the British could not see what they were going to do with this small territory where nothing would grow, where floods and typhoons raged regularly, and where malaria-bearing mosquitos were always prevalent. In general it seemed as inhospitable to human life as any place in the entire British Empire. Queen Victoria was reported to have been vastly amused when someone told her that she had recently acquired the territory of Hong Kong.

Within a few years, Captain Elliot was more than vindicated. Hong Kong provided not only an important military base for Great Britain, but a vitally needed port and trading post as well. Its usefulness as a military base has long ceased, but the city has remained a center of international trade and has, within recent years, become one of the busiest manufacturing and export centers in the world.

Hong Kong, like Venice and Amsterdam, is built on a series of peninsulas and islands. The sea water is its greatest asset and its greatest liability, because typhoons still sweep in from the ocean and flood the city with water during the monsoon season. This can be an enormous problem because while Venice has been losing population and Amsterdam's population has grown slowly in recent years, Hong Kong's citizenry has doubled and quadrupled. If masses really teem, they do so in the sweltering, humid climate of this city. And floods do not help.

Originally the prosperity of Hong Kong depended on one commodity: opium. Although the unlicensed sale of opium to China was illegal by treaty and international law, the British merchants who made their semipermanent home in the Crown Colony (Nobody ever expected to spend a whole lifetime in Hong Kong. One made a lot of money and left.), grew rich and powerful on the proceeds of opium sales. The Chinese government, appalled at what the drug was doing to its people, attempted to stop the trade, only to be caught up in the Opium War of 1839. The war started over a relatively minor incident: a group of British sailors became involved in a drunken fight with some local fishermen.

One Chinese was killed, and the Chinese demanded that the perpetrator be handed over for trial in a Chinese court. The British refused, and the Chinese retaliated by driving British citizens out of the nearby island of Macao. The war was on and was won easily by the British in about fourteen months. From then on the Chinese were powerless to combat the opium trade, which continued unabated for several decades, providing the British Colony with money and goods that increased its prosperity, a prosperity not shared by the Chinese population.

The Chinese and the British did not live in harmony. Hatred of the "white devils" who dealt in drugs, made their fortune and then departed was intense among the Chinese. In fact, in 1858, some of the local Chinese leaders hatched a plot to rid themselves of their foreign invaders for good: they decided to poison the yeast that the British used to bake the bread they consumed with their bacon, eggs, kippered herring and tea for breakfast. The Chinese did not eat bread and, therefore, the arsenic that was added in very liberal doses to the bread mixture was meant to kill off only the unwelcome foreigners. The scheme misfired. There was so much arsenic in the dough that the bread tasted vile and was not eaten. The few British men, women and children whose taste buds were not acute enough to detect the foreign substance received such large doses of arsenic in their first bite that they vomited the bread. As far as anyone knows, nobody died, although a number of Europeans had some fairly unpleasant hours.

Nobody was able to find the culprits who had hatched the poison plot. Some of the bakery owners were arrested but released when no evidence really linking them to the scheme could be found. Some of the bakery workers were kept in jail for up to three weeks, until it became evident that no one was going to incriminate anyone else.

In the long run, the plot only retarded Chinese administration of the city. The British had realized sometime before that they would be able to run the Crown Colony more effectively if they appointed an educated and loyal group of

Chinese civil servants to see to the day-to-day administration of Hong Kong. By the time of the arsenic plot, the British had completed a plan by which the administration, though not the control, of Hong Kong would gradually be turned over to the native population. But the indignation caused by the plot among the Europeans living in Hong Kong, and the pressure they exerted on the British Foreign Office in London, changed all this and probably retarded the growth of the Crown Colony for at least ten years.

By the beginning of the twentieth century, drugs were no longer the principal import and export of Hong Kong. In fact, the very Europeans who had so incensed the Chinese by their insensitivity to the drug problem were now worried about opium and morphine addiction among their own people. The addictive and deadly drugs that had formerly made their way into China were now finding a market in London, Paris and Rome. Ironically, today a large part of Hong Kong's city budget goes to combat the local drug trade, and much of this money comes from the British, who can ill afford to spend it, but who can afford the importation of illegal drugs even less. This is especially true since heroin, which is much more dangerous than raw opium or even morphine, is now the principal illegal drug making its way to European ports from the Crown Colony.

At any rate, by 1914, and the beginning of World War I, the British and the Chinese were living in an uneasy truce, made profitable by the unique trade situation in Hong Kong. It had been maintained as an open, duty-free port; and raw materials, manufactured goods and foodstuffs from all over the Far East made that small strip of barren land one of the busiest trading posts in the world. Chinese merchants were becoming fabulously wealthy, right along with their British counterparts, and no one in power on either side wanted to do anything that might destroy this mercantile gold mine. Yet there were still hundreds of thousands of poverty-stricken Chinese who never saw any riches at all. As Hong Kong grew richer, the poor peasants from the countryside flocked there, hoping to get a tiny share of all that prosperity. Civil unrest was frequent, but always use-less, since apparently money was a stronger bond than race or nationality. The rich Chinese made common cause with the rich British, and the poor never achieved the kind of power they needed to change their own miserable condition.

But Hong Kong was to change once again. In the 1930s things began happening that would, under most cir-cumstances, have destroyed a community that at best was maintaining a delicate balance in order to exist. The Japa-nese invaded China, and hordes of new refugees crowded into the already teeming slums of Hong Kong. The popula-tion, which had always been seen as overcrowding the tiny space, tripled and quadrupled within a year. Most of the British and other European merchants, who had left the Crown Colony at the beginning of the conflict between China and Japan, expected never to return. Hong Kong, they thought, was going to turn into a second Calcutta, a bleak hole in which overpopulation, unemployment, dis-ease and perpetual civil strife were the rule of the day. But the opposite happened. The Chinese merchants, who had never left, saw in the new immigration an unprecedented opportunity. Many of the Chinese who were the new refu-gees were professional men: engineers, managers and ac-countants. Many were skilled workers and craftsmen. If Hong Kong could not survive as a port after the end of the war (the Chinese, who had lived with wars for thousands of years, knew that peace would eventually return), why could the city not become a major manufacturing center? There was talent, cheap labor and an easy access to raw materials. The Chinese put all this to use. Industry in Hong Kong grew with every passing month. Today, almost as many goods made in Hong Kong pass through international markets as goods made in Japan or Korea.

Looking at the city today, prosperity still lives side-by-side with poverty. Hong Kong's streets boast some of the most luxurious cars in the world. (There are actually two gold-plated Rolls Royces belonging to a large industry that take important foreign VIPs from one of the most expensive hotels in the world to several of the most expensive clubs and restaurants.) But there are families living on old shipping trawlers in the harbor who are desperately poor and who don't know from one day to the next whether their crowded, leaky boats will support them for another twenty-four hours. There are slums in which twenty families share two tiny rooms, while children look with sick, hungry eyes at the curious foreign visitors who pass by to get a look at what the tourist guide calls, "The Chinese Hong Kong."

But all in all, prosperity seems to be winning. Because Hong Kong has become a business and tourist center, no one can really afford to allow urban decay to take over. So, inventive as usual, the Hong Kong civic leaders are putting a small percentage of their wealth into new housing, social and health services and other improvements that will keep the city in the kind of balance it needs to survive and prosper. Architects have found ways of building large housing developments on the steep hills that surround the city. Land that would be considered unsuitable for building almost anywhere else in the world is crowded with public housing projects, schools and hospitals—and the buildings are not crumbling into the sea as was predicted when the architectural plans were first published. In fact, in many ways Hong Kong city planners and builders are producing work that has become a model for construction on difficult terrain. There is little unemployment in Hong Kong, although most workers receive wages that would give a union leader in America or Europe apoplexy. Child labor has been banned in industrial plants, but there are still children as young as five and six working in small family-owned "factories," under conditions that no health code in Western industrial countries would permit.

There are other interesting contradictions in the city: until very recently the second largest department store in Hong Kong (and one of the largest in the whole world) was topped by a huge neon sign proclaiming in Chinese characters two stories high: "Long Live Chairman Mao." Right underneath in smaller blue letters was another sign in English: "We accept American Express Credit Cards." According to recent visitors to the city, the Chairman Mao sign has been replaced by another that just says: "People's Republic of China." The store management, in very practical Capitalist terms, had decided that naming various Chinese leaders might prove to be too costly—after all they seemed to change fairly frequently, while the name of the country remained the same.

Right next to the Chinese department store is another, even larger store, which belongs to an international combine that runs similar establishments in major cities. Sales help there make it clear that they prefer cash to credit cards, although after a brief argument, they will usually accept the latter.

Almost everyone in the city administration, from urban planners to garbage collectors, are Chinese. But the city still seems to be run in many ways for the foreign business representatives and tourists that crowd the hotels and office buildings. "We throw the book at anyone who picks the pocket of a foreign visitor," said a Chinese policeman. "We have to keep the streets safe for our visitors . . . or the city is in trouble. Crime in the streets, in the housing projects or in the industrial areas? Well, we have some very strict gun laws . . . but, on a Saturday night we do have a lot of violence among the local population. We try to solve those kinds of problems without throwing too many people in jail. Jails are expensive. But you know what one of our problems is these days? There are a lot of Japanese businessmen in the city. In the dark they look as if they are our own people, so if one of them is mugged, the mugger tends to tell us he just made a mistake. He wants to be treated more leniently, because after all, he didn't *think* he was committing a crime against a visitor." How did the policemen feel about courts that were more lenient when crimes were committed against their own people than against foreigners? When he really thought about it, he didn't like the system at all. But being practical, as most Hong Kong residents are, he too insisted that the city depended on the good faith and good will of the foreigners with cash.

Amsterdam and Hong Kong are very different from each other, but they have an important element in common: their leadership can adapt to varying conditions and varying times. They know how to use adversity to make creative changes. And change is a constant factor in a commercial society—those who can't change, or don't want to change, like the Worthies in Venice, may continue to own a lovely museum, but the world of business and industry will inevitably pass them by.

20

The Big Apple: New York City

CRISIS CITY:
PRICES: BIGGEST JUMP IN FIVE YEARS
MEAT: IT WILL BE SCARCE BY FRIDAY
GAS: THERE IS NO LET-UP IN SIGHT.

> Headlines, large enough to cover almost the whole front page of the tabloid newspaper the *New York Post,* June 26, 1979

New Yorkers, whose wide streak of solipsism* was reinforced during the years when this city's money troubles made it an international symbol for financial disaster, have had to adjust to the realization that all the really significant crises stirring the country seem to be happening elsewhere.

> *The New Yorker,* July 2, 1979, purchased at the same newsstand on the same afternoon as the June 26th issue of the *New York Post*

The fact that one can buy a newspaper and a magazine that look at New York City in almost diametrically opposing ways on the same day and at the same newsstand doesn't sur-

---

* 1 The theory that the self is the only thing that can be known and verified. 2 The theory or view that the self is the only reality.
The American Heritage Dictionary of the English Language.

prise most New Yorkers at all. They are accustomed to having New York praised as the greatest city on earth or damned as the filth and sin capital of the civilized world. New York is indeed a city of contradictions: the New York skyline features some of the tallest buildings in the world, yet, it also contains some small farms, and houses with large back yards and gardens. Some peoples of the world believe that New York's streets are paved with gold, but residents know they are frequently strewn with garbage or clogged with snow. Some residents live in large apartment complexes and don't know their next door neighbors. Others live in sections where active neighborhood organizations meet every week and everyone seems to be acquainted with everyone else. New York is supposed to be practical and business-minded. Yet it has one of the worst subway systems anywhere and the best ballet company in the world. What's more, the subways are getting worse, and the ballet is getting better.

Every other month the newspapers feature a new crisis: crime in the subways, endless lines in front of gas stations, a breakdown of the electric system, and most frequently, the threat of instant bankruptcy. Actually, New York manages to continue to survive admirably and attract some of the nation's most brilliant and ambitious men and women, some of the most idle and decadent, as well as some of the poorest and most desperate. Most people who come stay for decades. Whatever the city's problems, after having lived in New York for a while, people find that even the cleanest, best run, most sophisticated city in the world can seem somewhat dull and provincial. As one secretary, who had returned to the New York office of her company after a year in Geneva, Switzerland, put it: "Geneva is great if you don't want any problems and don't need any distractions. The streets are clean, you can walk everywhere at night without fear, the public transportation system is terrific, the people are friendly and helpful . . . and I was bored out of my mind." Three weeks later, she was complaining about all the problems in New York City again, but when asked

if on second thought, she might not want to return to prob-
lem-free Geneva, her instant answer was: "Heavens, no!"

Hundreds of thousands of people have seen New York
for the first time from an airplane flying over the brilliant
ribbons and clusters of light that are Manhattan at night.
Others have admired the skyline, which is as exciting a work
of man as anything that exists, from a ship passing the Statue
of Liberty in the New York harbor. And many of those
people tend to think of New York in terms of its most popu-
lous and glamorous borough: Manhattan. But there are
other boroughs: Queens, where Archie Bunker is supposed
to live, but which also has one of the outstanding public
colleges in the country (free to all who qualified, until very
recently); the Bronx where there are large, expensive private homes with a spectacular view of the Hudson River to
the west, and whole sections of burned-out, barren slum
areas with packs of wild dogs and cats scouring the streets
in the east; Brooklyn, where New York taxi drivers are
supposed to live, but where a lot of young stockbrokers who
commute to Wall Street offices also seem to make their
home; and Staten Island which, although it is an urban
borough, still has its share of working family farms. The five
boroughs, whose leaders compete fiercely for city funds, but
who can put up a united front in a minute when Washington's budget-cutters converge on the city, are connected by
an intricate network of bridges and tunnels, which clog with
traffic during rush hours and seem to be in constant need of
repairs for which, this year or any year, there just isn't
enough money. Yet, in the history of New York, no river
bridge has ever fallen down nor has a tunnel collapsed.

New Yorkers are supposed to be hardhearted, not concerned about their fellow human beings, sophisticated and
snobbish. Yet New York has one of the most generous and
humane welfare systems in the United States (although not
nearly as adequate as those in most large European cities),
and is one of the few American cities left with municipal
hospitals where those in need of care can get it free. New
York has been known at various times as "Fun City," "Sin

City," "Crime City," and "The Big Apple" (meaning a city of opportunity). Casual visitors from Kansas City and Kyoto wear tee shirts with "I love New York" printed on them. Most native New Yorkers would be much too embarrassed to proclaim their affection for the city in this way.

Instead, they may wear a small gold or silver-colored apple in their lapel or on a chain around their neck, and if asked why they happened to pick that particular ornament, will tell you that they just love apples.

The country at large has a love–hate relationship with New York City. The residents of Columbus, Ohio, or Altoona, Pennsylvania, may boast of the skyscrapers, the fine theaters and the great restaurants in New York City when visiting London or Paris; but they do not hesitate to write angry letters to their Congressmen in Washington every time another bill to rescue New York from yet another financial crisis is debated there.

We have all been accused of alternately romanticizing or criticizing New York City. Often we find ourselves doing both almost simultaneously. And that is not as surprising as it may seem at first glance. Because New York, while it has a great deal wrong with it, also has some very important things about it that are almost incredibly right.

For one thing, it's the one really cosmopolitan city on earth. It has been able to absorb people from a multitude of ethnic groups, cultures and races, not just with tolerance but often with a great deal of quiet planning and concern. Life may be simpler and more trouble-free in Stockholm or Zurich, but these cities do not have to cope with the diversity of population, race or even income and education found in New York. Istanbul, too, may be a cosmopolitan city, but minorities there have had a much more difficult time integrating themselves into the general population.

Citizens of London and Paris used to fault America in general, and New York in particular, for their treatment of blacks. This happened when those cities had only tiny minorities of non-whites, and these usually crowded away in dismal slums. Britain banned Indians and Africans from

England, even from its former territories in Africa and Asia, when more and more of these people fled from the tyrannies that overtook some of their third world countries. When Uganda, for instance, expelled large sectors of its Indian population, many of whom still had British passports, the number allowed to go to England was severely limited.

French Algerians did not always find an open-armed welcome in France, and Indonesians who moved to Holland when the Netherlands gave up that colony found that they too were not exactly received with enthusiasm. Of course, there are racial and ethnic tensions in New York, but compared with other Western countries and cities, America at large, and New York in particular, have accepted newcomers, sometimes with grumbling, but always with enough concern to make their lives better than it was before they arrived in the city.

One indication of how thoroughly various ethnic and racial groups have been accepted into the fabric of the city is to look at any city-wide election slate. It's a proverbial joke that there has to be at least one Italian, one Irish, one Polish, one black and one Spanish-American candidate on the ticket. (Lately, there also has been one woman.) In Istanbul, there are no Greek, Armenian or Jewish names on the city election roster; and very few East Indian, African or even Irish candidates offer themselves for public office in London. The joke that the ideal candidate for mayor for New York City would be a black nun called Mother Levy says something about New York that is both touching and partially true.

Of course, there is a great deal wrong with the city. There are areas in the South Bronx and in Bedford Stuyvesant that look like bombed-out war zones because the slums that festered there for generations have finally been abandoned or burned out. No one really seems to know what happened to the people who lived in those slums, but almost certainly they have not moved to more pleasant neighborhoods or better housing. There are people in New York who don't get even minimally adequate medical care;

youngsters who are intellectually normal, or even bright, manage to graduate from high school without learning how to read, write or do simple arithmetic; some men and women simply give up on life because they see no hope anywhere and wander the streets as vagrants. The subways are dismal, smelly, dirty, either overcrowded or under-used (depending on the time of day or night) and frequently unsafe. There are not enough policemen or firemen. Some buildings in New York have not been inspected for safety for decades, if ever. In June of 1979, a fire in Macy's, one of the world's greatest department stores, went out of control and killed a fireman because the sprinkler system, which apparently had not been checked in some time, didn't work. A few days later the granite and marble trimming on the exterior of another great store, which had moved into the building a few years earlier, came loose from the wall and crashed into the street, narrowly missing several pedestrians and a number of cars. A month earlier, a piece of granite had come loose from a building belonging to one of the world's great universities, Columbia, and killed a young girl. Obviously, no one had checked any of these buildings for flaws, simply because there are not enough people to do this kind of necessary preventive work.

Often New York seems to respond to problems only when a major disaster or a well-publicized incident occurs. For instance, the building and public health departments have known for decades that when any structure in the downtown area is razed, the rats that were almost sure to be there migrate all over the neighborhood. Frequently, appalled neighbors call the appropriate department only to be put off with promises that something surely will be done "soon." Soon often means never. But when a pack of rats from a demolished building attacked a secretary on Wall Street one May evening, some of the bystanders called a TV station, which sent reporters. Then, so many ratcatchers appeared on the block several hours later that it looked as if all the rats in New York were destined to become extinct within the next week. The only problem was that other rats in other parts of town continued to terrorize neighborhood residents, who were still being told that something would be done "soon." With no TV cameras on the spot, those rats could look forward to a long and healthy life.

There are potholes in New York streets that don't get fixed until election time, or until someone gets seriously injured and sues the city. Pornography shops, drugs and prostitution flourish in all areas of New York in spite of periodic vice raids, announced with great publicity and with TV cameras in attendance. Once the cameras have gone and the crusading city official has returned to his office to think of a new popular issue to publicize, the porno shops, drug pushers, pimps and prostitutes come right back . . . sometimes within hours of the well-publicized raid.

Americans in general, and New Yorkers in particular, seem to feel that these conditions are unique to their cities— that somewhere in the world there are large urban centers that don't have rats, or potholes, or uninspected buildings, or vice and corruption. Perhaps in a small, homogeneous country like Sweden or Switzerland, there are indeed such cities (usually with half the population of Staten Island alone), but in most cities of the world, the same problems exist and not nearly as many citizens are concerned about their solution. In fact, in spite of its well-publicized cynicism, New York is one of the most optimistic cities in the world: its citizens still firmly believe that problems *can* be solved with effort and creativity, and because of that belief, they often are.

Someone in Washington once made the rather obvious statement that problems could not be solved by just throwing money at them. That statement falls into the same category as another truism: money won't buy happiness. So, throwing money, especially if one doesn't calculate the direction in which it is tossed, will in and of itself not produce solutions. And money won't buy happiness, if a person is sick, lonely, selfish and generally uses the extra funds unwisely. But a person with enough money to live comfortably is more likely to be happy than one who is desperately poor. Urban problems, especially problems of a city the size of New York, will certainly not be solved by money alone. Yet much of what is wrong with New York could benefit from money, and much of what is right can only be preserved by money. Since New York, over the centuries, has sent much more money to Washington in various forms of income and other taxes than it gets back from all those lawmakers from states where miles of farmland and woods stretch as far as the eye can see, it would seem only fair and sensible to make sure that New York does not drown in money troubles. New York is one of the man-made wonders of the world. If the city is not worth preserving, what is?

4

WHY LIVE THERE? THE FUTURE OF CITIES

21

Fun and Games

The Main Event is the City Itself

> A headline in the *New York Times* over a story by architectural critic Ada Louise Huxtable discussing a museum show on "Urban Open Spaces"

Bread and Circuses

> That's all that the citizens of ancient Rome needed to keep them happy (and presumably, unrevolutionary), allegedly the opinion of Emperor Nero who, also allegedly, fiddled while Rome burned

Culture: a state of civilization, customs, especially a high level of development; improvement, refinement.

> *Webster's Handy College Dictionary*

Yesterday's city fun and games have often turned into today's cultural events. The classic Greek theater served as entertainment for the ordinary citizen of Athens, as did the Roman "games," in which gladiators fought to the death and lions ate Christian martyrs. The ancient Greek plays are still presented all over the world, translated into many languages, but we have substituted boxing, ice hockey, baseball and football for the Roman variety of games.

Wolfgang Amadeus Mozart was, for a brief and wonderful time, the most wildly acclaimed, popular composer in Vienna and Prague. In New York City in July of 1979, more than two thousand people stood in line in the rain for up to four hours to obtain tickets for the "Mostly Mozart" series of concerts that is given every summer at Lincoln Center.

Dancers, from the ancient Japanese court mimes to the whirling dervishes of Turkey, have always drawn crowds. They still do, as anyone who has ever tried to get a Saturday night ticket to the New York City Ballet, the Paris Opera Ballet, the Dance Theater of the Netherlands or the Stuttgart Ballet will tell you.

Musicians and poets may have written their most beautiful sonnets and love songs while looking at a starlit sky next to a burbling brook, but their publishers are almost always located in London, Paris, New York or some other major city.

As we look at the city scene today, only a very fine line divides popular entertainment of the fun and games variety from a cultural event. We really don't know which of today's playwrights, film makers, composers or writers will be considered the classic artists of tomorrow. But it's quite possible that in the year 2000 some colleges may be assigning the Beatles in a course called "Music of the Twentieth Century" and, almost certainly, English Departments will be giving seminars on the plays of Arthur Miller or Tennessee Williams. There will be Ph.D. theses on the choreography of George Balanchine in various graduate schools. It's even possible that Mohammed Ali will be the subject of biographies by learned scholars. TV's *I Love Lucy* may, after its apparently endless reruns are over, become the property of some museum interested in mass-culture classics.

At any rate, popular entertainment and cultural events have one major ingredient in common: They almost always take place in cities. Indeed, entertainment is probably one of the principal foundations on which cities are based. Humans are social beings. They like to get together in groups. And when they gather, they usually need something more than each other's conversation to keep from becoming bored.

We don't know exactly when one set of people called "an audience" first watched or listened to another set of people called "actors" or "musicians," because all of this occurred in prehistoric times. We don't know when a man or woman first put a collection of objects on view, decided they were worth preserving, and thus started the first museum. We don't know when the first builder, looking for beauty of structure and line, first used stone, sand, wood and mortar to create something that was not just useful but also, in his eyes, lovely, and thus became the first architect. But we can be quite sure that few, if any, of these events took place in isolation. Performers, whether they are painters, architects, actors, dancers, poets or musicians need audiences. Very few have been able to work in total isolation. And audiences are to be found in places where many people gather, *i.e.*, cities.

As an example, let's look briefly at the theater, which includes, of course, in our particular century, the movies, radio and TV. We know that as far back as 3000 B.C. the Egyptians put on ceremonies for funerals and for the coronations of pharaohs that set patterns still being repeated and refined. We know of the ancient court entertainments in China and Japan, the rituals of prehistoric Indian and African medicine men. Today, we would call these ceremonies, "plays."

The first recorded theatrical events took place in the fifth century B.C. in and around Athens, Greece. At first these events were also of a religious or ceremonial nature, but over the centuries, they were divorced from these roots and became, quite frankly, plays that produced tears or laughter (or both) and that left audiences feeling better about themselves and the world. The Greeks called this feeling "catharsis."

During the Middle Ages in Europe, the church frowned on performances that were considered to have no religious or moral value. But this did not keep playwrights,

Culture

Below: A cool and lovely garden is one of the pleasures that make life possible in even the most crowded, polluted city. The parks of Japan's cities are among the most beautiful in the world.

Right: A feeling of privacy is possible in even the largest city, as one lone skater in New York's Rockefeller Center finds out.

Far right: One of the pleasures of city life is to watch a great artist like Mikhail Baryshnikov dance. He's seen here at New York City's Lincoln Center. Photo by Costas

actors and audiences from getting together. Morality plays, in which the hero's virtues could be applauded and the villain, generally the devil, could be hissed, were performed outside cathedrals in towns and cities throughout Europe. Gradually this became the kind of play we now enjoy in the theater.

The Globe Theater in London was built in 1599. It was made entirely of wood, since in those days no one had as yet decided that public places needed some kind of fire code. In 1612 it was, as might have been expected, completely destroyed in a fire that demolished a whole section of London. It was almost immediately rebuilt, even before the city fathers had begun the reconstruction of official buildings, never mind alms houses or prisons. Londoners apparently needed a theater to cheer themselves up after the tragedy of the fire. The second Globe Theater was eventually demolished too; but, since the first Globe, London has never been without a center for popular entertainment. The Globe holds a special place in theatrical history because it served as the stage on which Shakespeare, Marlowe and many other great English playwrights presented their work. We may assume, however, that right along with *Hamlet* and *Romeo and Juliet*, there were some very forgettable and forgotten plays presented in those golden years of the British theater. It's in the nature of popular entertainment to produce some jewels and some disasters.

During the years that the Globe flourished, there were also smaller, less well known theaters in Madrid, Paris and Rome. In addition to the formal places of entertainment, wandering troupes of street players went from city to city, collecting audiences wherever they could.

The early Puritans who settled the eastern coast of the United States strongly disapproved of theatrical performances. There was little to entertain these rather dour souls except a hell-fire and damnation sermon in church on Sunday. It may be assumed, however, that some of the more picturesque and original preachers developed a following, just as actors and musicians did in other, less inhibited societies.

As America moved west, the barroom with its dancing girls probably served as the entertainment center for miners and cowpokes, but the citizens of more permanent settlements built meeting halls, which often served as community centers, schools and doubled as theaters to which entertainers of all kinds traveled. The small touring companies of actors and musicians that visited mining and agriculture towns of the Middle West and West were the logical successors to the street players of the Middle Ages.

It is not entirely clear when we started to make a distinction between entertainment and culture. Entertainment came to be looked upon as vaguely time-wasting, while culture was supposed to be good for you. Certainly, those Victorian young ladies who were taught to play the spinet and to sing (whether they were talented or not made absolutely no difference) acquired these skills to make them seem "accomplished," and therefore, more desirable marriage partners. This was culture. The people of Victorian times, not just in England but in most of Europe, encouraged the reading of earnest, learned tomes, while considering novels frivolous. No refined, well-brought-up young English lady visited a music hall, although a visit to the theater for a Shakespearean play was considered educational.

As was noted earlier, we have inherited much of our attitude towards entertainment and culture from the Victorians, along with our disdain for cities. One of the results of this is that we think culture is good for us while other forms of entertainment are, at best, neutral and, at worst, bad. So we construct so-called "culture centers" in our cities. These centers usually rise on inner-city land that was made available through slum clearance. New York City's Lincoln Center is built on land that formerly was considered a highly undesirable neighborhood. London's Royal Festival Hall (a huge complex consisting of many halls) is on a site overlooking the Thames River in which, during Charles Dickens's time, families lived in huddled tenements and thieves and thugs fought each other along rotting docks.

Movie theaters are moving to the outskirts, but theaters, concert halls and opera houses are built in the center of cities, with generous parking facilities usually provided to make it possible for the out-of-town folk to participate in all that culture. Has the system worked towards making the center of our cities more attractive, reversed the movement of middle-class families to the suburbs and improved real estate values so that city assessments and tax revenues can rise for a change? In some ways, the answer to that question has to be "yes."

Architects generally hate the cultural centers, whose buildings often contain lots of white marble and very little real style. This is what Paul Goldberger, critic of architecture for the *New York Times* had to say about Lincoln Center in his book, *A City Observed: New York, A Guide to the Architecture of Manhattan*. "Travertine (*ed. note:* a type of marble) here covers a multitude of sins. These are, for the most part, banal buildings, dreary attempts to be classical that took the form they did, not out of any deep belief in the values of classicism, but out of a fear on the part of architects that their clients, the conservative boards of directors, would not accept anything else. This is the progenitor (*ed. note* father) of every little 'cultural center' in every upwardly mobile city anywhere, from Maine to California. . . ."

Although Lincoln Center may be more pretentious than beautiful as architecture, it has been wildly successful as a true meeting place for some of the best music and dance available anywhere in the world. What's more, the space has lent itself surprisingly well to the combining of the kind of entertainment people seem to want with the kind of culture that's supposed to be good for them. Besides the operas, ballets and concerts that go on inside the buildings, the Plaza often attracts roving groups of entertainers, from jazz bands to folk singers, to dancers from every corner of the earth who perform free to a large and enthusiastic audience. For the past few years, the Plaza has also featured a crafts fair where one can buy anything from peculiar-looking pottery beer mugs and handmade penny whistles to lovely gold jewelry, hand-woven stoles and scarves, wood furniture of exquisite craftsmanship and elegant design, and even on occasion, a piece of interesting sculpture.

Other cultural centers in different parts of the United States have reported similar events. And many of the performances in the large marble halls are so fine that some city dwellers seem to have come to the conclusion that culture, besides being good for them, can also be fun. At any rate, tickets for the best of the ballet, opera and concert performances are usually sold out almost at the beginning of each season, and the seats in the upper reaches of the halls, where prices are still affordable, usually sell out fastest.

The centers have certainly done a great deal for the economic well-being of the areas surrounding them and have had the impact they were supposed to have on the cities' financial plights. Goldberger, much as he dislikes the architecture of Lincoln Center, has this to say of the project's money-making potential: "The economic impact of Lincoln Center has been enormous—this project may indeed break from sensible planning notions by exiling theaters into a separate cultural enclave, away from the rest of the city, but it surely worked in accord with urban renewal theory in terms of the effect it has on its surroundings. Property values have soared, and what had been a slum has become, for better or for worse, a place for the rich."

A place for the rich is right. The high rise apartment houses that now surround Lincoln Center rent for about three hundred dollars per room, per month. (Kitchens are counted as rooms.) Office buildings now being planned will rent for a lot more. But there's a place in the scheme of things for the not so rich as well. Almost every day, through spring, summer and fall, unless it's actually raining hard, young people from all over the city, the country and the world sit on the rim of the Lincoln Center fountain (phony classic though it may be) watching the passing parade of artists, tourists and just plain folks. The ice cream venders have a busy time, even though at eighty-five cents per serving that rum raisin or mocha almond cone is pretty expensive.

The seventy-eight-year-old woman, whom we shall call Mrs. Gold, can afford one of those cones per week, but she comes to Lincoln Center almost every spring and summer day, on the subway, from her model apartment for the elderly in Queens. Her ostensible reason is that she emigrated from Riga, Latvia, the hometown of her great hero, thirty-two-year-old dancer Mikhail Baryshnikov. She's never met the dancer, but she watches him as he goes to class at the School of the American Ballet, which is part of Lincoln Center, and in and out of the stage door of the New York State Theater, where he dances with the New York City Ballet. (In 1980 he will move to the American Ballet Theater, which performs in the Metropolitan Opera House, also part of Lincoln Center.) Mrs. Gold, who lives on Social Security, manages to see quite a few ballets, with or without Baryshnikov. She had never seen anyone dance, "except at a wedding" until she was seventy-four. "I'm the oldest groupie I know," she admits cheerfully as she crosses Lincoln Center Plaza to ask anyone near the New York State theater if perhaps they have a ticket to the next performance that they cannot use and would like to donate to her.

If she can't get a free ticket (surprisingly often she can), she will buy standing room. "It means I don't eat lunch, but who needs lunch?" Standing through three hours of a performance might seem like quite a feat for a woman of her advanced years, but she considers this an adventure. Usually, she manages to spot an unused seat somewhere in the orchestra before the start of the first intermission. She uses the pause in the performance to settle herself in that seat. The ushers all know her and applaud her initiative.

When the ballet is not dancing, Mrs. Gold still arrives at the Center early. She has by now learned to like classical music, and she transfers her attention to the concert halls

in Lincoln Center. "Very educational," she says approvingly.

"If I had not discovered Lincoln Center and Misha
(that's Baryshnikov to his friends), where would I be? In
that model apartment for old women who complain all the
time," she explains. "That's very boring. Now I look forward
every morning to the concert or the ballet I'll see in the
evening. Yes, I always manage to get a ticket. After all,
people feel sorry for old ladies like me. I don't mind that a
bit . . . let them feel sorry, just as long as I can get to see
Misha dance."

If it were not for Lincoln Center with its easy access
to both culture and entertainment, Mrs. Gold would indeed
be sitting in her apartment in Queens, worrying why her
son in Atlanta doesn't call more often. ("That's what all
the other women do . . . worry why their kids don't call.")
Out somewhere in the countryside, Mrs. Gold might by now
have literally been bored to death. Instinctively, she has
made the best use of the city in which she lives. She uses
what it has to give her: subsidized housing, a fast if not
always efficient or safe transportation system and the entertainment and culture that all add up to one word:
civilization.

22

Privacy and Community

Throughout history, people have moved to cities to find new jobs, new recreational activities and to participate in the larger community. Often they find one additional benefit: privacy. In places where there is a huge concentration of people, some individuals find it much easier to live lives that, in rural and suburban districts, might draw unwelcome attention to them, might cause them to be considered peculiar or at least unconventional.

From earliest times, those who have wished to live lives that did not conform to the standards set up by society have moved to the centers of large cities. In the country they might become the subjects of gossip and criticism. In the city, they are simply not noticed.

This fact was long ago discovered by artists, writers, musicians and others, who moved to specific areas of certain cities where they were allowed to follow the life styles that suited them. For the unconventional, the city has traditionally been a refuge from prying eyes and gossipy tongues. It is no accident that New York's Greenwich Village, Paris's Montmartre, London's Soho and other inner city locations developed their own colonies, right along with a reputation

for excitement, creativity, and usually, a faint tinge of somewhat loose behavior. In fact, the reputation sometimes became so strong and so attractive to tourists, who insisted
on guided tours through these art colonies, that the artists
found their privacy disrupted and moved on to yet another
part of the city. Greenwich Village today is no longer the
home for the many artists, writers, actors and dancers that it
was during the 1920s. Every summer, hordes of college
students who have read the memoirs of various artists
descend on real estate agents with requests for one of those
picturesque garrets in the Village. Presumably in Paris, a
similar group still seeks the artistic life in Montmartre. But
they are bound to be disappointed in both cities. The inexpensive garrets have given way to high rise apartment houses
with steep rents—indeed some of the steepest in the city.
The inexpensive neighborhood coffee houses, bars and
boutiques have given way to a variety of tourist-oriented
enterprises. Those now living in the former artist's quarter
tend to be young, affluent professionals who can afford air-
conditioned apartments with conveniences that the garret
dwellers could not pay for and did not need. The artists have
moved elsewhere. In New York, they may be rehabilitating
lofts in Brooklyn, in Paris they have probably gone on to the
working class suburbs. The same is true for the bohemian
sections of London, Florence and Munich.

But even when they do not live in special sections of
the city, city dwellers generally enjoy much more privacy
than country folk. Eccentric clothing or behavior that would
draw all kinds of attention in a village or a suburb, in the
city just disappears into the crowd. It's rare when a resident
of one of New York City's high rise apartments knows even
the names of the tenants on the same floor, let alone sees
them enough to observe their personal habits, or to criticize
their behavior or ideas. Certainly few are acquainted with
neighbors down the block or two streets away. Someone
would have to be flamboyantly eccentric to cause a ripple
in New York, Paris or London.

Even in those cities where members of families, or

former citizens of the same village still tend to congregate in one neighborhood—New Delhi or Istanbul, for instance —those seeking privacy tend to find more of it than they would in the countryside. Indeed one of the reasons many conservatives through the ages have been suspicious of city dwellers is that it is much more difficult to observe, criticize and control them than it would be if they lived in the more restricted society of a village or a suburb.

Of course, the privacy that the city provides also carries with it some lack of community protection and may give a sense of isolation. One of the principal objections that people through the ages have made to city life is that it carries fewer built-in emotional and physical support systems than village life. Everyone has a story about someone who moved to a city and was left in complete isolation when misfortune struck. There are certainly newspaper accounts of theft, murder and mayhem passing unnoticed in a city; and sometimes even when such incidents become obvious, neighbors refuse to get involved. There is a horrifying story of the murder of a young woman in New York City several years ago that was observed by more than a dozen people from their apartment windows. The victim screamed and tried to flee from her assailant over a period of at least ten minutes. He even left her once when he thought police were arriving on the scene, and then returned when it became obvious to him that no one would interfere. Not one of the onlookers tried to help the woman or even bothered to pick up the phone to call the police. When questioned about the incident later by shocked reporters, almost everyone indicated that either "someone else's trouble did not seem important enough to act" (i.e., "I did not want to become involved") or "I thought that someone else was probably reporting it," so that no action was necessary.

Of course, the case of the young woman was a particularly dramatic one; but some city dwellers, particularly the old, the sick and the emotionally disturbed can suffer alone because no one notices their plight. On an almost regular basis, TV news programs report stories of an old

man or an old woman who lives in misery and filth without
attracting any notice from neighbors, church members or
government agencies set up to prevent such situations.
Runaways can disappear in every city in the world without
anyone being able to find them.

But even such apparent indifference has, occasionally,
had its advantages. During World War II, the Germans
developed one of the most efficient citizen spy and informer
systems in history. First in Germany and later in the occupied countries, there were on every block and, occasionally,
in every apartment house, spies who reported on their
neighbors' ideas, reading materials, radio listening habits
and other activities directly to the German secret police,
the Gestapo. And yet in cities throughout these countries,
individuals and families were able to hide Jews, political
refugees and others sought by the Germans for months and,
occasionally, years. Anne Frank survived in a hidden apartment in central Amsterdam with her family for a long time
before a German police spy discovered the hideout and
reported it to the Gestapo. Anne Frank and all members of
her family except her father died in concentration camps,
but in other parts of Holland and even in Berlin, the capital
of Germany, some Jews survived the war years.

Only recently, the Israeli press told the story of one elderly woman who lived in the center of Berlin and sheltered
several young Jewish girls about the age of Anne Frank
through all the years of the holocaust. One of the points
made was that the woman knew few people in her own neighborhood because she had always chosen to live a rather
simple, isolated life. Since hardly anyone knew her, she was
able to hide the girls, obtain extra food and generally behave
in a way that would almost certainly have made her highly
suspect in a country village where her movements would
have been much more carefully observed by curious
neighbors.

It's also interesting to note that many revolutions and
other political upheavals start in cities, where preparations
can go unnoticed for a long time. Guerrilla armies may flee

to the hills when they are defeated or temporarily disbursed by hostile governments, but generally they begin their organization in crowded center cities where their activities can go unnoticed for months or years.

For individuals who need companionship and emotional support, city life can, of course, be lonely, especially for those who have moved to the city from a close-knit community in the country.

Many of the factors that can inhibit personal freedom in small towns—gossip, ostracism for unconventional behavior—may also provide a sense of belonging and warmth that seems absent from city life. After all, the person who gossips and condemns at least cares enough to take an interest, even if that interest is all negative. And to some of the lonely people who live in cities, even this kind of interest is occasionally welcome when there has been no contact at all with others in the neighborhood.

Some cities, however, do provide neighborhood support (right along with neighborhood nagging). In the cities of Turkey, New Delhi and other Far Eastern urban areas, people from one village who move to a city often try to find dwellings near each other, so that they can maintain the system of village closeness and support. And in some countries—Sweden and Germany, for instance—systems of neighborhood support are created by trade unions, churches and the government. Some cities in Germany have a formal system known as "Notnachtbar" ("neighbor in times of trouble"). Everyone in an apartment house or on a block is assigned a neighbor, to work on a kind of buddy system. The neighbors are supposed to call each other fairly regularly to make sure that no emergency has occurred that requires assistance. And if an emergency arises—an illness in the family, a death, or for that matter, even a broken stove or refrigerator—everyone feels quite comfortable about calling the Notnachtbar for help. Often, if a person is too shy or too proud to ask for help, someone in the block or in the building who knows who the assigned helper is will call that person to say that assistance is needed.

One of the reasons the system seems to work so well is that those who help out know that next month, or next week, or perhaps even the next day, they might have to call for assistance, and that the person whom they are helping today will be ready to help them tomorrow. It is highly unlikely that the young woman who was murdered in New York would have met a similar fate in Bonn or Dusseldorf. Someone would have alerted the Notnachtbar, and the police would have been on the scene within minutes.

So city life, while offering the advantage of privacy to many of us who find this quality important in our lives, also produces a sense of helplessness and isolation in others. But systems are being developed either formally, like the Notnachtbar in Germany and the block associations in New York, Chicago and San Francisco, or informally, to break through loneliness and to offer community assistance when needed. Eventually perhaps, we will be able to have the best of both possible worlds: a chance to live our lives as we see fit without concern for what the neighbors think or say, along with the kind of help all of us need occasionally from the community.

23

The Americanization of the World's Cities

. . . the thirty-year-old American lives in a house that was built when he was twenty.

These houses are too young to seem *old,* they seem merely outdated to them; they lag behind the other tools: the car that can be traded in every two years, the refrigerator or the wireless set. That is why they see their cities without vain sentimentality. They have grown slightly attached to them, as one becomes attached to one's car, but they consider them as instruments rather than anything else, instruments to be exchanged for more convenient ones.

For us a city is, above all, a past; for them it is mainly a future, what they like in the city is everything it has not yet become and everything it can be.

> French philosopher Jean-Paul Sartre, in an essay on American cities, written in 1955

In the lobby of the only large hotel in Katmandu, Nepal, music by Musak is playing "Truckin" by the Grateful Dead and "Mrs. Robinson" by Simon and Garfunkel. At the main ferry dock in Hong Kong, a group of young men and women, wearing imitation Levi blue jeans, is selling the genuine article for seventy dollars per second-hand pair. Somewhere in the desert near Amman, Jordan, an architect is planning a hospital. It looks faintly familiar to anyone who regularly takes the train from New Haven to New York. It should. It's an almost line-for-line copy of the new Harlem Hospital, which passengers see out of train windows just before pulling into the 125th Street Station in New York City. The Hilton hotels in London, Istanbul, Berlin, Cairo and points east, west, north and south are, with the exception of a few "native" touches, almost interchangeable. There are Holiday Inns in Italy, Denmark and in a few other European countries.

Outside of Kyoto, Japan, within walking distance of one of the most beautiful Zen temples in the world, is a shopping center that features Dunkin' Donuts, MacDonald's hamburgers and Kentucky Fried Chicken. One might mistakenly believe oneself in a shopping center near Wichita, Kansas, except that the picture of the bearded gentleman decorating the chicken store looks more like Charlie Chan than the Kentucky colonel.

An office building that might just as well be standing somewhere on Park Avenue in New York City, or in almost any other large American city, can be seen from several angles behind St. Paul's Cathedral in London much to the dismay of many who love the old city as it was. A huge skyscraper, very much like one in Houston, Texas, obscures the magnificent harbor view in Hong Kong. A hotel that looks like a convention center anywhere in the American Midwest can be seen at the very top of the Mount of Olives near Jerusalem.

In 1955, philosopher Jean-Paul Sartre may well have pondered the differences between American and European cities, but by 1980, American music, clothing, cars, and most of all, building and planning techniques were obvious everywhere in the world, with the possible exception of the remoter parts of Tibet. Even in Peking a number of American industries are planning large new plants (the latest is Pepsi-Cola), and one may assume that they are not going to use ancient Chinese building techniques to construct their factories. An American hotel chain has already asked to build several large tourist centers in China and Russia. The Americanization of the world's landscape is in full swing.

Sometimes, American technology can indeed help to solve some pressing problems for other countries. For instance, when the housing shortage in and outside of Paris became so acute that, unless one was a member in good standing of the international jet set, one had to wait years to find an affordable apartment, the builders and architects of Long Island's Levitt Town were asked to build a few thousand housing units as quickly and inexpensively as possible in a suburb of Paris. The construction did provide new homes for a great many young French families, although again, architectural critics were not overflowing with enthusiasm at the sight of all those identical units.

In Turkey, tourism has become the one sure source of much-needed American dollars, German marks, French and Swiss francs, and one may presume, a certain amount of Arabian gold. But, until very recently, there were simply not enough hotels in even the major cities to accommodate the hordes of visitors. On some of the choicest potential tourist sites, the Turkish Riviera with its endless sandy beaches, featuring Greek and Roman antiquities in the dunes, there were no hotels at all. If one did not want to camp, bringing all one's own necessities—there were no official camp grounds either—one just did not go there.

In recent years, hotels, looking very much like smaller versions of what might be seen in Miami Beach or along the coast of California, have been sprouting up along that coastline. Most are not built by American companies (Germans and Italians seem to have taken advantage of these particular business opportunities), but the plans are either designed by American architects or they are fair copies of what can be seen every month in issues of the latest American architectural and/or interior design publications.

Imitation may be the most sincere form of flattery, but often the Americanization of a very non-American landscape seems inappropriate at best, and ugly or dangerous at worst. Often the planning does not suit local conditions. This is particularly true of buildings and installations that are more important to the health and welfare of a country than a hotel or an office building, or a Pepsi-Cola plant.

For instance, in several of the less developed countries there are few hospitals in major cities and even fewer in the countryside. As governments are becoming more concerned about health problems, hospitals are being built. Often they turn out to be copies of health centers in major American cities. In a desert oasis, a ten-story high hospital makes very little sense. In American and other large overpopulated cities, it seems logical to save needed ground space by building vertically. But in the desert, where space is unlimited but electricity and other technological necessities are not, building a hospital that requires an elevator is wasteful and, frequently, self-defeating.

A country that has very few rural schools might be better served by one room schoolhouses than by a replica of the latest regional high school in Westchester County, New York or Orange County, California. But planners who have learned their skills from recent publications, and teachers familiar with the latest technology probably never heard of the one room schoolhouse.

Our highway system works well in our own country, where transportation by automobile and truck is the chosen method of moving goods and people. In a country that still uses donkey carts, bicycles and an occasional 1932 rebuilt motor vehicle, a six lane highway is expensive, useless and dangerous.

Along with our technology we have exported water and air pollution. The clouds of acrid smoke over Ankara or Cairo can be seen ten miles away on a clear day, and the waters around many Black Sea ports are no longer useful for fishing because the fish have died.

Often the American government or industry has sent experts, at the request of the government of a developing country. These experts have pushed American products, building techniques and ideas. One of the most damaging

American customs that has spread into undeveloped countries is the use of canned or powdered baby formula, instead of breast milk. These formulas are advertised widely in those countries as being convenient and safe. Somehow, many of the mothers have received the impression that this form of artificial milk is better for their infants than mother's milk. The result has been an epidemic of infant diarrhea and other bacterial diseases, which have damaged and even killed thousands of infants.

The problem, of course, is that in a country where there is little safe water, few facilities for sterilization of bottles and nipples and no refrigeration, the infant formulas that can be prepared safely and easily in a developed country become a breeding ground for deadly bacteria. It seems ironic that in this country with all our advanced technology, medical experts are beginning a concerted campaign to convince American mothers to breast feed their infants, because breast milk is better than the most superior manufactured product in most cases. In other countries, where breast feeding was the only method of infant nutrition until a decade ago, salesmen are trying to convince the local population that American technology is somehow superior to Nigerian or Ethopian or Jordanian mother's milk.

Some of our "experts" are also influencing life styles and production in other, not very constructive ways. For instance, Turkey has what might be considered a very adequate railway system, particularly for a country where much of the technology is still relatively underdeveloped. Certainly the train that runs between Istanbul and Ankara (a part of the justly famous Orient Express, which only recently abandoned some of its Balkan schedules) is one of the most luxurious, cleanest and most pleasant in the world. The number of times it has been late within the past ten years can be counted on the fingers of one hand, according to the stationmaster in Istanbul who has been on the job for over thirty years, and who seems to know every nut and bolt on those trains. Yet, the "expert" sent several years ago to help the Turks improve their rail

Guess Where?

Most cities of the world now have sections that look as if they came straight out of the latest American architectural magazine. Guess where some of these buildings are located.

Nowhere, USA. A façade of any American city at Universal Studio's motion picture lot in Hollywood.

On pages 252 and 253: Stockholm, Sweden. Swedish Information Service

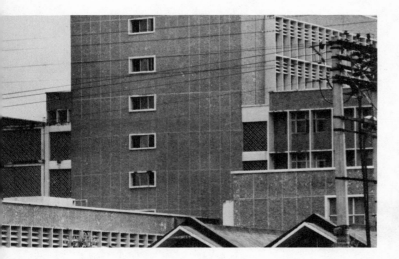

Jerusalem, Israel

New York City

Hong Kong

Luxor, Egypt

Istanbul, Turkey

New Delhi, India

system between Istanbul and Ankara was an executive from an American railroad that, in spite of a great deal of U.S. government assistance, has gone bankrupt several times. What's more, a stationmaster at Grand Central Station would probably have to use the fingers on both hands, plus all his toes, to count the number of times the trains were late in the course of a single week. One can only hope that the people in Ankara who have to listen to advice from American experts of this kind don't understand English, and that the Americans don't speak Turkish, with no translator available for the duration of the visit.

However, there is a great deal our technology can do to help solve problems: our own and those of others. Certainly some of our medical techniques have helped to wipe out some of the world's worst epidemics, most importantly smallpox. We have helped to turn malaria-infested swamps into fertile acres. Our poisons have killed many of the rats that carried bubonic plague and our sprays have killed the lice that transmitted typhus.

American plant genetics and fertilizers have made it possible to grow more grain and rice and vegetables in places that were formerly arid. Providing more food on fewer acres is an accomplishment of which we can be proud.

Our building technology has helped some countries provide shelter and establish industry in ways that work for those countries. Our road-building skills have helped to make formerly inaccessible spots accessible. And certainly blue jeans, whether made by Levi or some factory in Hong Kong, Russia, Germany or France are a practical and generally attractive garment.

The reason for the popularity of American music all over the world is that our records do seem to strike a spark in young people everywhere, even though Elvis, the Grateful Dead and Kiss probably puzzle elders elsewhere, just as they do in this country. Apparently, people in other countries enjoy Kojak, The Fonz, and even such golden oldies as Sergeant Bilko and *I Love Lucy*. At any rate, one can watch those shows in Arabic, Finnish, German and Japanese. But often, when we export our culture, our technology and our life style, what's best about us stays at home and what's worst and least useful becomes the local fad in cities from Iceland to Uganda.

As we have seen, the American city has its problems as well as its advantages. We have little control over who adopts what in the rest of the world. But perhaps, one of these days, it might be worthwhile to send "problem experts" overseas. These experts might advise other governments about which of our difficulties have been caused by adopting ideas that looked like easy solutions and instead only complicated the problems. In many ways, we might be able to help others most by informing them of the mistakes we have made along the road to progress. If the Americanization of the world, particularly the less developed countries, proceeds unchecked, we may find ourselves in a world where too many cities are facing identical problems at the same time, and the net result may turn out to be chaos.

24

*Cities
of the Future*

The bureaucratized, simplified cities so dear to present day city planners and urban designers and familiar also to readers of science fiction and utopian proposals run counter to the processes of city growth and economic development. Conformity and monotony, even when they are embellished with froth and novelty, are not the attributes of developing and economically vigorous cities. They are the attributes of stagnant settlements.

Jane Jacobs, *The Death and Life of Great American Cities*

Hidden away in the northern Arizona desert, not far from Two Horse Cordes Junction, a supersonic city structure called Arcosanti rises from a bleak and beautiful mesa. Eerie half domes called apses range across a ridge top and 40 feet high vaults complete the unearthly panorama. An abandoned set for the filming of *Star Wars?* Not quite, but the planned Arcosanti community will be no less futuristic.

The first full-sized project of architect and philosopher, Paolo Soleri, Arcosanti embodies the principle of "Arcology," a new way for man to build and live in natural surroundings. Arcosanti will eventually be a self-sufficient, non-polluting metropolis that grows vertically rather than horizontally, combatting urban sprawl without sacrificing open space and other comforts.

Bob Henschen, in the magazine *Festivals*, 1977

Any city planning worthy to be called organic must bring some measure of beauty and order into the poorest neighborhood.

Lewis Mumford

We may assume that since the first group of prehistoric families moved into one community, there have been those who felt that city life could be improved. Through the ages, philosophers, writers, architects and painters have constructed in their minds the ideal city, which would have every advantage of urban life and none of the disadvantages.

Although city planning as a profession is a development of the latter half of the twentieth century, a few cities were indeed planned: Paris, New York and Washington, D.C., for instance. Some just grew like an organic garden: Mexico City, Lima, London, Berlin, Istanbul and Jerusalem, to name a few. There is some evidence that planning worked better than no planning, although even planned cities seem to share the problems of the unplanned ones. But no one has as yet come up with a foolproof city plan, and no one probably ever will. Cities are complicated organisms. They represent, after all, a concentration of the single most complicated organism in nature: the human being. So they share collectively all the contradictory qualities of the human race. Cities represent our highest aspirations: concern for our fellow man, desire for beauty and our wish for peace. They also represent some of our other, less admirable drives: greed, hostility, superstition and a general ability to pollute every environment in which we settle.

The city of the future will probably be flawed like every city of today. But there are some problems we will have to solve or we will destroy our urban areas and the rest of the planet along with them. For instance, during the past few years we have finally reached the inescapable conclusion that our sources of energy are finite. If we keep on using oil, wood, natural gas and even coal at current rates, we will use up all we have by the time our great-grandchildren have grown into adults. Cities in the developed world have based their growth on the availability of unlimited supplies of energy. That attitude will have to change. Meanwhile, cities in the less developed world are attempting to base their futures on the same sources of energy that those in the developed world have been abusing for generations. They, too, will have to be convinced that in spite of the bad example that has been set over the centuries, they will have to use alternative methods of powering their industry and agriculture.

Within the past few decades almost no topic has been discussed as extensively as the future planning of our cities. Blueprints range from ideas as simple and achievable as the reestablishment of old neighborhood patterns, advanced by such social critics as Jane Jacobs, to the construction of super-cities in space by such visionaries as philosopher and architect Paolo Soleri. Between these two extremes are a variety of architects, sociologists, planners, economists, politicians and even a few writers, all of whom have suggestions as to how we can make cities more viable and more beautiful in the future. Let's look at a few.

Jane Jacobs believes that the old, unplanned cities with their strong neighborhoods had many advantages that we have overlooked as we put into motion grandiose plans to clear the slums, rebuild our downtown shopping areas and generally reorganize city life. She has always seen the city not as a gigantic whole but as a series of relatively small, interlocking communities, each taking care of its own members, but also contributing to the overall welfare of the total society. To her, the grandmother sitting on the porch stoop in Baltimore, New York or Philadelphia is a better deterrent to crime (and certainly to juvenile mischief) than the most mechanized police force in the world.

The parish priest, or even the local nosey neighbor, she feels, is often a better person to help in crisis situations than the uptown welfare department with the experienced professional social workers and complicated computer systems. She believes in the neighborhood school, the neighborhood grocery store and the neighborhood doctor and lawyer who know the people and their problems as no outsider could, no matter how highly skilled.

In the past few years, especially as federal urban renewal programs have bulldozed neighborhoods and often created more social problems than they solved, her point of view has found a great many supporters. Among them is Senator, and urbanologist, Daniel Patrick Moynahan, who has said that he occasionally prefers the old-fashioned political ward heeler to the more modern and antiseptic reform organization. The ward heeler knew if there was sickness or unemployment in a family, if the husband drank and beat his wife, if one of the kids was getting into trouble, if the rent was months overdue. And often, he was able to help, exacting political favors, of course, in return. He could provide a few shovels of coal during a cold wave, a turkey at Christmas when there was no money, a job for Uncle Fred who seemed to spend his time hanging around the pool hall and a good heart-to-heart talk with Fred's nephew who looked as if he was about to follow in his disreputable relative's footsteps. The friendly, disembodied voice from the local Reform Democratic Club that reminds everybody to get out to the polls on election day can perform none of these functions, Senator Moynahan has maintained. He is not for bringing back the political bosses with their corruption and dictatorial powers, but he would like to see some new system that would take over some of their more helpful social functions.

There are architects and planners who work hard at preserving neighborhoods, often battling real estate operators and others more interested in profits than people. The whole idea of recycling buildings is taking hold throughout the United States. In the older cities of the world, an interest in preserving neighborhoods is also taking hold. Areas of Paris, London and Rome are being revitalized, along with whole sections of Washington, D.C., New Orleans and New York.

The danger in some of this type of revitalization is that in some ways, it can become too successful. As sections like Georgetown in Washington, Brooklyn Heights in New York and Trastevere in Rome become attractive, they also become fashionable and expensive. Often the result of revitalization is similar to bulldozer renewal. The people who formerly lived in the neighborhood are driven out by the high-priced, rebuilt accommodations, which only the rich can afford. Neighborhood patterns are destroyed just as surely as if the buildings had been torn down instead of refurbished. Some planners are now beginning to make sure that at least a goodly percentage of those who formerly resided in the revitalized areas will be permitted to remain in their newly improved old homes.

But, along with those who want to preserve what's best in the old, there are those who plan for the really new. For instance, there is Israeli architect Moshe Safdie, who wrote a book called, *For Everyone a Garden.* The title would lead one to believe that what he had in mind was moving city populations out to the countryside, or at least the suburbs because that is where the gardens are, right? Wrong, says Safdie. Gardens can be anywhere, but they should be in urban areas because that's where we need them the most.

Safdie analyzed a number of cities, including Tokyo, Paris, Rome and Moscow. He listed the various activities that go on in cities and then estimated the volume of space needed by each activity. He found that most cities operated in completely irrational patterns. Much of the street space was taken up by automobile lanes. Cars moved in the open air, people moved inside buildings (either on stairways or in elevators) and frequently used underground passages to get from building to building or across the street.

One of the reasons for this pattern, he decided, was that the buildings were constructed vertically with one story cutting out the daylight from the other. Streets, whether used for cars or people, were built horizontally and took up most of the available light and air. Would it be possible, he wondered, to build huge, open structures made up of three-dimensional lattice-like sections in which people could be moved on open, horizontal conveyors, instead of closed vertical ones? The buildings would include their own "streets" with shops, theaters, libraries and schools as part of the overall open pattern. Around the buildings would be garden-like spaces. Cars and other forms of transportation would move underground.

He tried out his concept at the now famous "Habitat," built for an international exposition in Montreal, Canada. The building proved to be highly successful, although very expensive. He is attempting similar plans now in various other cities and feels that openness, air, greenery and space must again become part of the cityscape. So far, his concepts have only been tried on a very small scale, but he hopes that when larger scale projects get under way, construction methods, using prefabricated parts, will become less expensive and, therefore, more feasible.

Occasionally, architects and planners get the opportunity to plan and build a city where there has never been one before—Brasilia and Ankara, for instance—or to reconstruct one that had been destroyed by a natural or man-made disaster. Usually, such efforts tend to be not very successful. A city that looks marvelous on the drawing board may turn out to be unlivable. Generally though, architects and planners have been more successful at rebuilding cities that have been destroyed than creating brand new ones.

We have already discussed Ankara and Brasilia, which were designed by a series of different planners. Some have said that the reason for their generally antiseptic, unlived-in look and their many flaws in even the simplest kind of social and economic planning (the lack of sufficient water in Ankara or the unemployment in Brasilia) was that no one person had the overall responsibility for their creation. But there is at least one city designed by one man who is one of the greatest twentieth century architects, Le Corbusier. Chandigarh was built on a seemingly endless plain in India

after that country won its freedom from Great Britain. Its
elected ruler, Jawaharlal Nehru, wanted the city to express
the vitality and creativity of the new country. By almost any
standard, the effort was a failure. Nehru gave Le Corbusier
almost complete freedom and, at least theoretically, an
almost unlimited budget to plan the ideal city. It turned out
to be a series of monumental buildings with vast empty,
paved spaces between them. The enormous concrete structures connected by paving and an occasional artificial lake
look somehow inhuman. Of course, the city was never completed. The unlimited budget turned out to be an illusion,
as such budgets usually do. India, after all, is a very poor
country with enormous unsolved problems. But even if we
use our imagination to fill in the many empty spaces, the
city does not work. For one thing, the architect apparently
felt that a completely flat site was not suitable for the kind
of monumental architecture he had in mind. He created
large numbers of artificial mounds, which screen off the
flatness and the extent of space around. They give the whole
enterprise the look of a stage set for an opera by Wagner,
with gods and goddesses cavorting among the granite monuments of an ancient time, or of a propaganda ballet by
Russia's Bolshoi company with eager workers hammering
away at the future. It does not look or feel like a city in
which men, women and children will live, eat, sleep, play,
work, be born and die. In a strange way, Chandigarh is
just not ordinary enough. It has remained, throughout decades, what it apparently was designed to become: a
monument, rather than a living, breathing, developing city.
Because Le Corbusier was one of the greatest architects of
this century, the failure of Chandigarh seems to prove that
it takes more than theoretical ideas to make a great city:
it may take the ideas and experience of those who have
lived in that particular place to create a comfortable as
well as a usable place.

Rotterdam, Holland, was almost completely destroyed
by bombs during World War II. The entire center city had
to be rebuilt from the ruins, and for a number of reasons,

the rebuilding project turned out to be exceedingly successful. The Dutch, as we have seen in their planning and
construction of Amsterdam, seem always to be immensely
practical. The Dutch also, unlike most of their European
and American contemporaries, have always put the automobile second to the pedestrian and the bicycle on their
schedule of urban values. This has proved to be both practical (building highways and wide roads costs money and
wastes precious city space), ecologically right (gasoline
fumes pollute the environment), and beautiful (parks and
gardens are more pleasing to the eye than concrete roads
and parking lots).

The center of the new Rotterdam is almost entirely
pedestrian. Rows of two-story, small shops line the streets,
which are connected by a series of mini-parks. Yet, over
the low-rise shopping district, one can see high-rise office
and apartment towers indicating that one is not in some
picturesque country village, but in a very real urban setting.

Instead of granite and marble monuments to celebrate
the beauty of city life, the planners of Rotterdam have used
the commodity for which Holland is famous: flowers. The
flowers add color to the cityscape, and they also indicate a
progression from one street to another. The Dutch landscape architects use these flowers the way some of our most
sophisticated, modern graphic designers use signs: to indicate a change of function and pace. Masses of red tulips
and roses indicate that we are in one section of the downtown shopping center, masses of yellow blossoms that we
are in another, and a whole group of white flowers shows
that we have turned yet another corner.

The new Rotterdam is livable as well as beautiful.
Unlike most new towns, instant cities and other urban areas
created in a few years to accommodate thousands of people,
Rotterdam has a chronic housing shortage. It seems as if half
of Holland would like to move there. So perhaps Rotterdam
gives us one lesson for the future: we have to consider how
the city of the future looks, of course, but we have to be
even more aware of how the people in the city of the future

will *live*. Monuments are fine for museums, but for everyday life, they are often more depressing than inspiring.

When another of this century's great architects, Eero Saarinen, wrote about the city of the future, he had never seen the new Rotterdam. His book, *The City,* was published in 1943 when the center of Holland's great seaport was in ruins. But he must almost certainly have believed in the principles of those who eventually directed the reconstruction of the Dutch city when he wrote: "I have tried to visualize the present city's gradual evolution toward the city to come, always retaining the human and living side of the problem as the leading theme. That is, I have endeavored to picture the city of the future as the home city of the population in the same spirit as a house must be made the home of a family if it is to be livable and socially constructive."

Saarinen added another thought: "the practical city planner tends to think of present needs. He considers his colleague who thinks of the future as a prophet, or even worse, as a professor, who has never had to meet a payroll." Yet, who is really more practical, the man who builds only for present needs, ignoring the fact that they will change, or the one who takes present needs into consideration but also keeps his mind on what the future might bring? Saarinen believed that the practical businessman and the visionary would have to work in some kind of partnership to produce cities that would not just be beautiful but livable in the future.

Certainly the "practical" planners who built glass towers with no moveable windows in American and European cities because heating and air-conditioning had made it unnecessary to allow any city air to enter, must have had second thoughts in the summer of 1979. In the United States, President Jimmy Carter directed everyone to set their air conditioners at seventy-five degrees. When the sun beat down on the glass walls, many air-conditioning systems simply could not function at that high a temperature, and the inside of some of these "practical" buildings hit a

sweltering ninety degrees. Even if a lovely breeze was blow-
ing outside, those working in the glass towers got no benefit
from it, since no windows would open. The "practical"
planners who built these airless towers because moveable
windows are more expensive to install than fixed glass could
not even envision a society in which energy could become
so scarce that running air-conditioning systems all the time
would not only be wasteful and expensive, but illegal.

In coming winters when icy winds and sleet will be
hitting those glass walls, and when there will probably be
a limit on the amount of heat we will be able to use, we
may learn the same lesson: ignoring future possibilities is
not practical, it's wasteful and stupid.

No one has ever accused Paolo Soleri of being practical. Indeed, his name is usually preceded by such adjectives
as "Utopian" or "visionary." He has designed cities that
probably will never be built. Some, instead of being anchored
in the firm earth, literally float in the sea or are built on
some kind of space platforms. He dislikes most present
technology, the free enterprise real estate system, suburbs,
shopping centers, skyscrapers, housing developments and
automobiles. When one adds it all together, one might come
to the conclusion that he actually dislikes cities. He says
he does not. But his ideal communities in many ways re-
semble small way stations or, at the most, country towns,
though some of his projections are supposedly large enough
for one million people. It is interesting that he finances some
of his visionary research with the sale of wind bells, which
are designed and manufactured in a very small plant in
Scottsdale, Arizona. The one large-scale building project
he has undertaken is the town of Arcosanti, built in the
mesa country of northern Arizona and expected, eventually,
to have room for about three thousand inhabitants. The
construction of Arconsanti began in 1971, and to date there
are fewer than two hundred people living there. Most of
these are students who not only volunteer their labor but
also pay tuition in order to spend six weeks helping the
master realize his dream. Almost all the construction work

(as well as the cooking, cleaning, filing, typing) necessary for a construction project is done by volunteers. Other funds are raised through an annual festival, which features rock music, lectures, art shops and other cultural events. This usually draws a few thousand Soleri fans to his experimental community.

It's easy to dismiss what this planner is doing as completely irrelevant to any kind of normal city life. After all, no one expects New York, London, Rome, Lima, or even Hoboken, New Jersey, to run on volunteer labor, or to be financed by rock concerts or by the sale of wind bells. But much of what Soleri plans and does is interesting, and it may well turn out to be a good deal more relevant than anyone suspected, even ten years ago.

Soleri was one of the first planners to talk in terms of ecology, to predict shortages in fossil fuels, such as oil and coal, to warn of the dangers of air and water pollution and the serious health problems the disposal of chemical wastes could produce in some of the most crowded urban areas on earth. He was using solar energy long before it became a pop concept, was making do with locally available building materials before transportation became a real problem. He found ways of making his model community self-sufficient without the use of automobiles before the price of gas climbed to over a dollar a gallon.

There have always been Utopian planners whose ideas for the most part seemed eccentric, if not downright strange. But, more often than not, some of their ideas could be adapted in a variety of ways to real urban needs. There is a good chance that some of what is happening in Arcosanti may in fifty years be not only useful but necessary for those planning our largest urban areas. As Saarinen put it: "The visionary and the practical businessman will have to reach out to each other, will have to work together to keep our urban planet green, and to maintain its people with some degree of safety and dignity."

But cities are not going to be saved by the rich, the powerful and the super-educated alone. Probably many of us who love cities and who want to live in them will have to use our heads and hands, our imaginations and our knowledge to make our particular part of the urban planet a better place for us all. There are the block associations in New York and Chicago, the neighborhood patrols in some sections of Rome, the Notnachtbar of Cologne and Bonn, the village elders of Istanbul and the grandmother sitting on the stoop supervising everybody's grandchildren in Baltimore or Jerusalem or Mexico City. Occasionally, there is a person or a group of people who have what seems like a small and simple plan that can turn a tiny part of a slum into a garden.

In New Haven, Connecticut, one woman had such an idea. Betty Phillips is an unusual social worker. She helps patients in an inner-city psychiatric clinic deal with their daily problems. Many of those she tries to help are women, most of whom are very poor and feel overwhelmed by powerlessness and isolation. They worry about their rubble-strewn neighborhood, called The Hill. It was once prosperous, but recently a city official called it "a great slum surrounding a great University" (Yale). What Betty Phillips felt her little corner of the urban problem needed was a project that would unite people, would give them work they enjoyed, a chance to create something beautiful and useful and, as an extra bonus, a solution to at least one of their problems: their need for fresh, nourishing food, which they often could not afford to buy.

Since the city planners seemed not to be doing anything about some rubble-strewn acres that bulldozers had cleared for some unrealizable urban development project, she felt the land should be put to use. The people in the neighborhood could get together and plant acres of vegetables: carrots, corn, peppers, cabbages, potatoes, tomatoes. They could have a joint project that would release each family from its crippling isolation. The neighborhood would certainly look more inviting, as a result, and the individuals in the project would feel that they had some power to change something about their lives. To top all these other benefits, everybody would finally have a decent diet instead of subsisting on day-old bread, canned spaghetti and the junk foods their children somehow managed to buy at the small local markets.

She wrote a proposal asking the city to turn over the land to a non-profit neighborhood corporation. "Plotting Utopia, Acre by Acre," she called it. The city fathers were only too delighted to get rid of some of their blighted land. She asked for a small foundation grant and received enough money for seeds, fertilizer, garden implements and the salary for one experienced community organizer with skills in farming. At first, during the early spring months of 1979, only a few women in the neighborhood showed up to clear the rubble, stone by stone, from those ugly city lots. But they were soon joined by more of the neighbors and by dozens of children who arrived after school to help. At the beginning of the planting season, rows and rows of vegetables and flowers were set out on several acres.

As the season progressed, all kinds of helpers suddenly appeared on the scene. The city park department arrived with expert advice and additional plants. The fire department, during a dry spell, offered the use of a hydrant and the loan of an unused hose to water the gardens. A local group that specialized in Latin American music offered to play a benefit to get more money for needed supplies and equipment; and some evenings, they just set up their instruments and played for the neighborhood people who were hosing and weeding the land, lending the whole neighborhood the kind of festive air it had not experienced in decades.

In the fall, the people of the Hill harvested their city crops. From the state's department of agriculture came advice on how to can extra vegetables, how to store potatoes and carrots through the winter, and how to prepare the vegetables so that the youngsters, accustomed mainly to hamburgers and Cokes, would agree to eat them. Somebody suggested exhibiting some of the vegetables at a country fair. "I think we grew one perfect tomato," Betty Philips said proudly.

Next year, the farm acreage is expected to double. But what may be more important is that those who live on the Hill are taking a second look at their dilapidated houses and their deteriorating community. Perhaps with a little paint, a little sweat and a lot of determination and hope, the dying neighborhood might yet be revived.

One perfect tomato may seem like a strange beginning for the salvation of a neighborhood, or a city, or of our tired, dilapidated urban planet, but it's one first step taken by a person who believes that the city can be improved through individual efforts. Multiply that thought and that hope by millions, and our urban planet will have the chance for the future it must have if all of us are to survive in a civilized world.

Index